DISCOVERING
PLACE

Readings from Appalachian Writers
Fifth Edition

Ernest Lee
Carson-Newman College

The McGraw-Hill Companies, Inc.
Primis Custom Publishing

*New York St. Louis San Francisco Auckland Bogotá
Caracas Lisbon London Madrid Mexico Milan Montreal
New Delhi Paris San Juan Singapore Sydney Tokyo Toronto*

McGraw·Hill

A Division of The *McGraw·Hill* Companies

Discovering Place
Readings from Appalachian Writers

McGraw-Hill's Primis Custom Publishing consists of products that are produced from camera-ready copy. Peer review, class testing, and accuracy are primarily the responsibility of the author(s).

 3 4 5 6 7 8 9 0 BKM BKM 9 0 9

ISBN 07-014343-9

Editor: Judith T. Ice
Cover Design: Mary Ellen Congleton
Printer/Binder: Bookmart Press

Table of Contents

Section III: A Sense of Place in the Family

Some Notes on Authors / 197

Acknowledgements

Wilma Dykeman, from *Explorations* by Wilma Dykeman, 1984. Reprinted with permission of Wakestone Books.

George Ella Lyon, "Literature in Its Place", first appeared in Mossy Creek Journal. Reprinted with permission.

Jeff Daniel Marion, "Wren in the Window", "The Man Who Made Color", "Ebbing & Flowing Spring", "The Egrets", "The Man Who Loved Hummingbirds". Reprinted with permission of the author.

Harry Middleton, from *On the Spine of Time*, copyright © by Harry Middleton. Reprinted by permission of Simon & Schuster, Inc.

Parks Lanier, "Writing About Literature". Reprinted with permission of the author.

Guy L. Osborne, "O, Appalachia: Artists of the Southern Mountains". Reprinted from *The Appalachian Journal*, Summer 1992, Vol. 19:4 with permission of the author.

Wendell Berry, "A Native Hill", "To Know the Dark" and "The Wish To Be Generous" from *Recollected Essays*. Copyright © 1965, 1980, 1981 by North Point Press. Reprinted with permission of Farrar, Strauss and Giroux.

Wendell Berry, "In This World", "A Standing Ground", "The Peace of Wild Things", from *Farming: A Hand Book*. Copyright © 1969 by Wendell Berry. Reprinted by permission of Harcourt Brace & Company.

William L. Bevins, "Stories, Myths, and Personal Identity". Copyright by William L. Bevins. Reprinted with permission of the author.

Pat Salyer, "Clinging to the Roots", "Muddy Creek Ritual". Copyright © by Pat Salyer. Reprinted with permission of the author.

Barbara Kingsolver, "Homeland", from *Homeland and Other Stories* by Barbara Kingsolver. Copyright © 1989 by Barbara Kingsolver. Reprinted by permission of HarperCollins Publishers, Inc.

Rick Bass, "River People", "Shortest Route to the Mountains" from *Wild to the Heart*. Copyright © 1987 by Rick Bass. Reprinted by permission of Stackpole Books, Mechanicsburg, PA.

Larry Cook, "Opening Day". Reprinted with permission of the author.

Jeff Daniel Marion, "The Wayside Diner", "Fishing at Emert's Cove in Late Fall", "Boundaries", "The Farm Wife's Aubade". Copyright © by Jeff Daniel Marion. Reprinted with permission of the author.

Jeff Daniel Marion, "Crossing Clinch Mountain in February" from *Tight Lines*. Copyright © by Jeff Daniel Marion. Reprinted with permission of the author.

James Still, from *River of Earth*. Copyright © by University Press of Kentucky, 1940, pages 71-77. Reprinted with permission of the publisher.

James Still, "Heritage", "Leap Minnows, Leap" and "Death of a Fox", from *The Wolfpen Poems*. Copyright © Berea College Press, Berea, KY 1937. Reprinted with permission of the publisher.

Preface:
A Note on Appalachian Writers and the Text

The writers in this book are Appalachian in the sense that their lives and imaginations have been influenced by the people, the traditions, the images, the geography, and potentially any other of the characteristics or distinctions that are what we may term Appalachian. Some of the writers live and work in Appalachia, while others who may not live in the region now have been affected by it either through direct experience or by heritage. Their works selected for this book obviously are diverse, but the writers do share a common theme concerning the process of discovering one's place (see the following introduction to the student).

I want to offer a special thanks to my friend and colleague Jeff Daniel Marion for his invaluable advice and assistance in selecting authors for the text and to my colleagues in the English Department at Carson-Newman College for their support and suggestions. Also, I wish to pay tribute to Angela Roberts for her dedicated work in preparing the manuscript, to Joy Hayes for her work as a student editor, and to Judy Ice, Chris Bowie and the staff at McGraw-Hill for their kind assistance and support.

To the Student:
An Introduction to Appalachian
Readings and the Art of Writing

The immediate purpose of this text is to serve as a collection of models for improving your writing and appreciating more deeply the art of writing, which actually means to appreciate yourself and your world more profoundly and with more excitement. These readings are not intended primarily as studies of literature, but rather as samples of the process of the art of writing, as samples of powerfully expressed feeling and thinking. The broad theme which unites the varied readings in this text is a sense of place, which is a major theme in modern writing, an apparent need for which we strive in a world that is obviously more and more fragmented and dislocated. For you as college students, the need to establish a sense of place for yourselves is vital, and it is a pressing concern for you particularly if you are newly arrived on campus and will be necessarily involved in attempting to achieve a sense of place, of belonging here, as well as striving to establish a sense of place for yourself as an independent, thinking adult in the society toward which you are moving.

For any thinking person, the struggle truly to gain a sense of place is a progressive, life-long experience. And certainly this struggle to feel a sense of place is a major one for writers who have lived or are living in the Appalachian region, an area of the country that has experienced profound changes in the environment, the family, religion, etc.--as has most all of America. In a 1977 symposium addressing the problems of living in the Appalachian region of America, Loyal Jones, a leading teacher, thinker, and writer in Appalachia, concludes: "But what seems important to me is to preserve or to create within ourselves a sense of independence, self-reliance, duty, a feeling of place, for family, for persons, for personal integrity" *(Appalachian Heritage.* Summer 1977, 56). It is my belief that one of the most reliable means we have for preserving and creating this vital sense of place is through our reading and our writing, and it is the purpose of this text to offer us samples which will serve both as writing models and as springboards to thinking and writing and experiencing which will help make this course more than just another college course, but rather an unforgettable experience that through writing and thinking and keeping your eyes open will vitally involve you in life, especially life here and now in this place.

You will note that the readings are grouped under the broad theme of a sense of place, but are further subdivided under the recurring themes of discovering a sense of place as a writer, a sense of place within nature and the community, and a sense of place within the family. These themes are ones which I know to be good ones for developing writing topics and for drawing on one's experiences and moving to new experiences. The writing samples are drawn primarily from writers who live in the Appalachian region--writers from Tennessee, Kentucky, Virginia, North Carolina, and other area states. My purpose is to begin with writings about places and experiences which may be close to your own places and experiences and, when considered in league with other readings and considerations in the course, may serve to demonstrate the universal nature of experience and of the writing process. I hope to bring writers to you so that you can learn from them, find a sense of kinship with them, and realize that memorable writers ultimately do not just write about a region or a subject: they are involved in life and so life is involved in their writing, whether it be a short story, an essay, or even a business letter.

Ernest Lee

Section I

The Writer's Sense of Place

Wilma Dykeman
from *Explorations*

A long time ago I became acquainted with a young man (who eventually became an older man and has since died) who was a scholar in the truest sense of the word. He held a responsible position in one of the major oil companies but did not seek the highest executive positions--because "his" time, the hours and days away from his desk, were spent in his studies of mathematics, the history of science and enjoyment of music. His pleasure and great wealth was of the mind.

A few years ago I met a retired banker who had moved his residence from the northeast to the Southern Appalachians. He appreciated, indeed he loved, the mountains and on any walk or hike with him he observed each plant and tree, moss and shrub, asking for names, habitat, characteristics. His curiosity was as boundless as his enthusiasm for his adopted place, and I often compared his concern with the apathy shown by many natives who did not know, nor care to know, about the magnificent world around them.

A few days ago I encountered this sentence in a book I was reading: "The purpose of research in every field is to set back the frontier of darkness."

Let us give the word "research" a broad and spacious interpretation. The doctor in the laboratory is pushing back the darkness of sick minds and bodies; the scientist at his calculations is pushing back the shrouds of space; but each of us, as well, when we sharpen our minds, respect the gift of our curiosity, and seek to know more about this world and this adventure called life--we are overcoming our own bit of the darkness.

As an English novelist once said, "I like to understand things because then I can enjoy them. I think knowledge should intensify our pleasures. That is its aim and object, so far as I am concerned."

How right he is! And yet how dreary many of us consider knowledge to be. Its acquisition is made laborious, when it should be joyous; we plod toward something called learning when we should run and skip and plunge, stumble and rise and run again. Not that research of any kind, and knowledge worthy of the name, does not require work. But it is work repaid not only in earning of bread but in winning of our very spirit.

Perhaps we too often mistake facts for knowledge. As an eminent archaeologist has pointed out, the kind of unrelated scraps of information one gets on a quiz program offer scant satisfaction. "Bare facts by themselves do not fascinate us; they must be clothed with the play and counterplay which produced them. The defeat of the Spanish Armada in 1588 is a bald historical fact. It takes on meaning when it is shown as the culmination of a play of forces and the clash of the opposing temperaments and philosophies of two nations, personified in the characters of Philip the Second and Elizabeth. To understand these antagonisms, one must know the cultural backgrounds, the ways of thought, and the conflicting traditions of the two peoples. One must study Torquemada and Chaucer, John of Austria and Latimer, the choir stalls of Toledo cathedral and the fan-vaulting of St. George's, Windsor, and even the dances and field sports of the protagonists."

All knowledge then is related. When we know more about the corner of the world where we live, we know more about the green and fragile planet which is home to all humans. Our own little spark of curiosity is a part of the immense mystery which surrounds all life.

To know! To seek to know! How dull and dead we are when we relinquish that right, that rapture in our lives. Whether it is in mathematics or music, woods-knowledge or earth-wisdom, or effort to understand ourselves and those around us-- whatever the area of our knowledge, how satisfying to realize that truly "the purpose of research in every field is to set back the frontier of darkness."

Jeff Daniel Marion
Wren in the Window

While I scribble the morning's
words, she weaves a twiggy nest
with moss and thistledown,
snuggling into her tucked away
corner between sill and screen;

I remember last Spring's nestlings
nurtured in this river-cradled window
and one gray morning in May lost to the black
snake skilled in scaling walls:

now she hops to the ledge,
ruffles her feathers in a shrug.
I shuffle through the leaves
of a notebook, my tangled nest
of words hopeful but wingless.

George Ella Lyon
Literature in Its Place

With the publication this spring of *Common Ground: Contemporary Appalachian Poetry*, ninety poets from the mountain portions of six states will come into print together. Some are established writers with several collections to their names; others are just starting out. Like the region they share, their voices and perspectives are varied, echoing Virginia Woolf's struggle to "make of the moment something permanent," as well as Mother Jones' motto, "Pray for the dead and fight like Hell for the living."

Common Ground is a landmark book, for in it a people so often defined from the outside--pitied, praised, rehabilitated, dismissed--speak for themselves and do so in that most concentrated and direct form, poetry. But will the book receive the critical consideration it deserves? Will it, assuming adequate distribution, be taken seriously in American letters?

I have my doubts. Flannery O'Connor writes in *Mystery and Manners* that "the best American fiction has always been regional," and we might argue that for poetry as well. However, we know that whenever critics label a work *regional*, they imply that it is provincial or minor. No one calls the New York poets *regional*, though to the extent that its writers are shaped by their place, identify with and chart their imaginations by it, New York is a literary region as surely as Appalachia or Yoknapatawpha County. Yet our longings for sophistication are such that we respect the most arrogant urbanites extolling their place while we laugh at a Kentuckian who declares in a political ad, "I'd rather hear the rooster cry on Sookie Ridge than ride the subway in New York City." *That*, we say, is provincial.

It is funny, too. How could he want to stay on that ridge facing another rim of mountains? How could he not want to travel, to ride the subway daily, his landscape the same scrawled-over ads? Each world has its journey, its constricted vision. The difference is that people on the subway are perceived as *going somewhere*, part of a society moving onward, upward, while people on Sookie Ridge are perceived as *staying*.

It is un-American to stay. The pioneer moves on. There are new territories to explore, new places and people to find, and there is always much that is old to get free of. "Quit writing about the past," an editor once advised me. "The past is a fad." Though we've settled ourselves to the crumbling edge of the Pacific, though we've staked our claim on the moon, we still feel that need to slough off "the old country" in the form of Idaho or Alabama, to be rid of our native speech from West Virginia or East Tennessee. This was brought home to me recently when I gave a reading at a university on the edge of the mountains. Afterwards a graduate student told me, "Your poems sound so familiar. My parents speak broken English too." *Sheesh.*

This student, like so many of us, went to school to learn who she was and to forget where she came from, to construct a future by cutting herself off from the past. To be called Appalachian, like the poets in *Common Ground*, would seem to her self-defeating. Her origin was what she had to overcome. She had a university accent now--slightly southern, but that could not be helped. Wanting to write, she was headed toward Culture, somewhere she'd be close to the literary scene.

There is something to be said for her attitude. First, she has to learn of the world outside her gate, since she is also its citizen; and she has to learn who she's not in order to find out who she is. Second, in practical terms, if she gets to the centers where publishing is done, where writers and their business are a lively part of things, she has a better chance of conventional success.

But there is danger in this attitude, too, perhaps the gravest one a writer faces: the danger of losing the voice she's denying, of writing on stilts, high above her "cultureless" place. Wendell Berry examines this dilemma in "A Native Hill." Kurt Vonnegut, too, takes it up. "No matter what your first language," he tells us, "you should treasure it all your life...I trust my own writing most, and others seem to trust it most, too, when I sound like a person from Indianapolis, which is what I am. What alternatives do I have?"

The alternatives are all forms of falsifications: to sound urban when you're rural, English when you're American, white when you're black, male when you're female, bluegrass when you're Appalachian. This is not to say a writer has only one voice or is limited to the scope of her backyard. But in some sense her work must begin there, at the rootwad. And wherever she travels she must take that place with her, must feel in the dark of memory for its shape. If not, her work will be the literary equivalent of Walter Cronkite's accent: literature from nowhere.

Perhaps some would consider that the ultimate sophistication--to be beyond place, to be culturally out of this world. But who would listen to us from that pure realm? Who in the world of road signs and groceries would be touched by that clean, well-lighted voice? We might as well seek truth from the telephone computer which tells us, "The number is..." or expect welcome from the Atlanta airport simulated guide, "You are entering the People Mover. There will be no food or drink beyond this point."

No food or drink. No cornbread or borscht, no moonshine or Manhattans, no Goose Creek or Yonkers, Honey-Eatin' Richard or Papa who played the horses at Santa Anita. Remember those food pellets we thought the astronauts would bring us from their voyage into the future? They were to give us all we needed from eating-- except pleasure, creativity, history, ritual. Likewise, literature freed from the spirit and limitations of place is solipsistic, without community.

Because of the triumph of their work, writers such as William Faulkner, Eudora Welty, Carson McCullers, and Flannery O'Connor are no longer called regional but Southern, clearly a step up. But less well known writers from the same province are still dismissed in the critical courtroom, just as the poets of *Common Ground* are likely to be. A writer is guilty of regionalism until his reputation (not his work) proves him innocent, whereupon someone decides that his place, rather than being remote, is universal. Eudora Welty points out the folly of this in "Place in Fiction":

> "Regional," I think, is a careless term, as well as a condescending one, because what it fails to do is differentiate between the localized raw material of life and its outcome as art. "Regional" is an outsiders term; it has no meaning for the insider doing the writing, because as far as he knows he is simply writing about life.

Is a life lived in Paris more significant than one lived in Nebraska, a tragedy in Chicago more important than one on Troublesome Creek? That depends on how deeply the writer has seen and how well she knows her task. We have Colette *and* Willa Cather, Richard Wright *and* James Still. We don't have to categorize and rank and exclude; we have only to go where they will take us. And the worth of the journey is not measured by the type-size on the map. It is the human heart we are traveling, always a rugged landscape. Where life is lived deeply into language, where it draws its strength from native ground, however far it may branch into sky: that is the place for literature. We do not measure it by population or industrial growth, by the presence of a philharmonic or a subway. We measure it word by word where we find it, by what it makes us see and think and feel.

For literature, the witching wand is no less than the whole receptive self. Will we say it's not water because it doesn't flow from a faucet twenty stories up? Will we reward sameness until we find ourselves on Interstate America, existing only to drive through McCulture, "over 90 billion sold"? Or will we travel different roads and listen to many voices, telling us we are together but not the same; we are rich and varied and distinct? That is the vision Walt Whitman offered in "Song of Myself": "One of the Nation of many nations, the smallest the same and the largest the same/... I resist anything better than my own diversity/ Breathe the air but leave plenty after me,/ And am not stuck up and am in my place." We hear that diversity in the poets of *Common Ground*. May we welcome the gift they give us of ourselves.

Harry Middleton
from *On The Spine of Time*

Preface

It is autumn and the night is clear and cold. A great dome of stars stretches across the sky as though pulled down tight over the worn, dark ridges of the Great Smoky Mountains. The stars give the night sky a pale white glow, like light reflecting off melted candle wax.

It was a good day along the creek. Just before noon, the sky turned black as wet coal and it snowed hard for hours, a great whirlwind of snow, and still I fished.

Snow was soon piled up on the backs of dark, smooth stones, and the sudden cold, the unexpected turn of weather, stirred me as much as it did the trout. I had almost forgotten how much fun it is to fish the high country in a good snowstorm.

I have lit the stove, put a pot of chili on. Staring up at the great sprawl of the mountain night, my back snug against a broad maple, I realize again that what I see is like the reflection in a rearview mirror. We see the universe not so much as it is, but as it was. The light I see in the blue-black mountain night, even of the stars closest to the earth, is old light, old news, light that is already more than four years old by the time I see its faint glimmer. Yet, to me, to my eye and senses, it is immediate and urgent, the topography of the present moment, a wild dance. Meanwhile, beyond my view, if not beyond my imagination, beyond this brilliant mountain night illuminated by spent starlight, the universe continues to reel from its inception, the original Big Bang, continues to expand like a blind worm probing through dark soil, alive only so long as it moves.

It is touch and go, whether it is the insect larvae snug beneath the flat-backed stones at the bottom of the creek or distant galaxies adrift in the dark belly of space. It is all dilemma and no final answers. Thank the gods.

It's all touch and go.

Almost all the leaves are off the trees. They scuttle about the ground, rattle in the cold wind: the year's excess spent, exhausted. Up higher, up above 5,000 feet, there are still the bold greens of the great dying fir and spruce forests of the Canadian Zone, but here midway up the ridgeline of the mountains, winter is a study in the latitude of grays and browns.

From the stony brow above my campsite, out on the rippled lip of the ridge, I can clearly see the lights of Bryson City, North Carolina, down in the valley. The lights look like flecks of mica shining in some fold of wet, dark soil.

Tomorrow, even if the trout rise, I will have to pack up, move on, hike back down the mountainside, and head home, back to the hills of Alabama. I lack Horace Kephart's wild courage and his resolute happy madness. Something compelled him to walk away from one life, including a successful career as one of the nation's most respected and learned librarians, plus a wife and family, and a host of attendant obligations, and into another world and life in these mountains. He never looked back.

While the chili cools down, I look down into the valley and see the lights of the houses and know I must go in the morning. There is a mortgage to pay off, a car with a worrisome cough and balding tires, the usual heap of bills. The radio in my study doesn't work. I need to fix it so that late at night, I can turn the dial to hear how humanity is doing. There is the squirrel in the attic that I haven't been able to evacuate. I've tried everything, even a bucketful of mothballs. I need to get back, put on my headlamp, lay the sleeping bag on the roof, and wait the squirrel out, discover how it comes and goes.

Comes and goes.

I need to get home--for a time, anyway. I have two sons. Both expect to go to the college of their choice. There is a cat that depends on me, too, and a month's worth of laundry to do, and a lawn my neighbors expect me to keep tidy and well groomed. There are taxes to pay and moral commitments and work piling up on my desk.

And so on.

These mountains are fickle and change with each slant of light. The world I see in one range of pale violets is another world entirely in the first pools of morning's hazy blues. Things don't end so much as fade, dissolve, disappear, and reappear as something altogether different. Even the mountains come and go, affirming the wild rhythm of possibility and tendency rather than certainty. Tomorrow at sunrise I will break camp along the rushing waters of the creek, and head down the mountainside toward town. I left my car at the Deep Creek campground. It's the grimy brown one in need of a good wash and wax. When I get to the campground, I will look back up at the mountains as I always do, see them rising up out of the morning's thick blue fog. Sometimes they remind me of lifeboats, there for anyone wanting to feel the palpable touch of solitude and solace against his skin.

A few words of explanation on this cold and windy mountain night. This is not a book about the history--social, cultural, or otherwise--of the Great Smoky Mountains or the high country of southwestern North Carolina, which is where most of the high country trout streams that haunt and soothe me are located. Neither is this some great quest or sojourn, nor a chronicle of some ambitious pilgrimage, angling or any other. It is not an angling guide to the trout streams of the Great Smoky Mountains. There are hundreds of miles of excellent trout streams in these mountains. The best advice I can give is this: come. Park your car. Listen for the sound of fast water, trout water, and start walking.

This is just a story of mountain creeks and streams, of mountain trout, of mountains and mountain people. It's a look at life, its losses and joys, its tragedies and happinesses, what is lost in a life and what is found. There happens to be a lot of fishing in this story, as well as certain slants and ranges of light, and time spent well and spent foolishly, perhaps. Mostly, though, this is a story of people--people I have met in these mountains. Some brushed against me like a wind, touched me, and were gone; others have happily become, almost accidentally, a great part of my life.

I began going into the Great Smoky Mountains and into the nearby Slickrock Wilderness and Snowbird Mountains more than a decade ago. I was on my way to West Virginia and got sidetracked. Lucky me.

As a boy I began keeping a journal. I was in other mountains then, the Ozark Mountains of northwest Arkansas. I have been filling up journals ever since. It's an affliction. Writers suffer from all kinds of afflictions. (Healthy and rational people who think they want to be writers should consider some other, perhaps saner, line of work).

Each night, I scribble endlessly in my journal, putting in everything--stolen conversations; people's appearances and habits, also conscripted without permission; the day's weather; what I've seen and what I've imagined; what I've felt; joys and sorrows; prejudices; the fragile state of my personal economy; wonderings; newspaper and magazine clippings; what I'm reading of late and whether or not it's worth the trouble; grocery lists and car mileage; playing backbone Delta blues in Onward, Mississippi; spending the night at Muleshoe, Texas; the solace of mountain streams, fast water, moving water; trout hooked and trout lost. Everything.

A good deal of what I write about comes from my journals. They hold what I want to remember, including my travels among these mountains. Much of this book was first written in the rough form of daily recordkeeping in my journals. The people in this story are real. I have fiddled with them, changed some things about them, such as their names, their appearance, and so on. Nothing more. All of them are more real than imagined.

Was there really a man who played bagpipes along Hazel Creek? Yes, though I never discovered who he was or why he stopped coming to play his music along the creek. I wish he would come back. I miss him.

Was there a man who walked about the mountains carrying a prayer wheel, offering a free spin and hope of a kind to everyone he encountered? Yes.

Rachael Settle's dog is really named Dog. And so on.

This is what Arby Mulligan said when I told him I might put him in this book, "Just say that anyone who's not afraid of a little ice-cold mountain water on their head is welcome in the Church of Universal Harmony, and there's no charge and no obligations. As for readin' and interpretin' the bumps on their heads, well, there might be a small charge."

This is what Tewksbury said, "Make it clear, dear friend, that I find it immeasurably easier to make money than to angle for trout."

Bob Winterwolf Dougal was too nervous to comment. He has a chance to attend the Wharton School of Business of the University of Pennsylvania. But he has nightmares that if he does his soul will turn white. He is full-blooded Cherokee: a fine Native American, a fine man, as complex and delightful, exasperating, and haunting as every Native American I've been honored to know, beginning with Elias Wonder, the old Sioux who lived in the shack along Starlight Creek, down from my grandfather's farm. Elias Wonder was gassed in World War I and everyone thought he was a lunatic who would torch their farms or scalp them in their sleep. He was the sanest man I've ever known.

Truth has a befuddling quality about it, even in the deep quiet of the mountains. It's like quantum physics. Sooner or later you've got to let loose of certainty's hand and leap. Jump. Believe in something, like mountains and mountain streams, trout and mountain people.

Harry Middleton
from *On the Spine of Time*

Crossing Over

It is early April and the window is open wide. A cool wind fills the small room on the second floor where I keep my des   k, a lamp, a chair, and floor-to-ceiling bookshelves packed with books. From where I am sitting, near the room's only window, I can see the moon. It is a little short of full and its reflected light gives the night sky a brooding cobalt-blue coloring. The moon itself is a blend of benign yellows with a muted green mist that hangs at its edges like a ragged halo.

A glaucous moon. That's what I called it yesterday in trying to describe it to a friend of mine who is a disenchanted physicist, a man I often turn to, seeking the answers to difficult questions. I asked him why moonlight and some areas of the night sky seen from the nearby Smoky Mountains sometimes appear tinted by this lovely pale olive-green light. This is what my friend the physicist told me: "Toxins."

"Toxins!" My voice rose in disbelief, a blend of moan and wail.

"Sure," he said in an even-tempered voice. "Airborne toxins. Billions of tons of them. The atmosphere sags under their weight. So do our lungs." He got up from the kitchen table, began searching through the icebox. "Say, does a beer come with this inquisition?" he said. His voice had the warble of birdsong. "All this talk of toxins gives me a powerful thirst. They have such a hard, metallic taste about them."

My friend the physicist has a way of never cheering me up. He used to drink bourbon instead of beer, but he had to give it up, he says, because these days two drinks make him want either to fight or cry. Three drinks and he speaks French, a language he cannot recall ever learning.

"Yep, toxins," he said again, the can of beer hissing menacingly as he popped the tab.

Toxins: the word seeps about my brain, bores into the soft cinerous tissue, laying open tangles of braided nerves. Tonight, staring out the window at the moon, the nerves in my brain rattle and flinch at the dismal irony that such a gorgeous moon, such an alluring light, might be the product of heavily polluted air.

Should one of my sons ever ask me about the color of dying air, I will have an answer, quick and sure. This is what I will tell him: murderous yellows laced with impotent greens.

An hour ago the wind shifted. Now it is blowing slightly north of east, straight out of Mississippi. Odd how things seem to have trouble taking hold in Mississippi, even the wind. I know the feeling, though: that almost inexplicable restlessness of the blood that seizes the muscles, claws at the nerves. Impatience stalks me at every season, settles in my gut--a knot that refuses to give way. It nibbles at my flesh, an emotion like schools of tiny fish whose hunger is insatiable.

Each day's light brings the sudden urge to travel, to undertake some fresh journey. Strangely, exotic destinations do not haunt me. These days my wanderings always lead to the same place, the Great Smoky Mountains. Standing at the window, I strain my eyes hard to the northeast, out over these Alabama foothills, and tell myself I can see the great, worn, rounded peaks of the Smokies, massive shadows rising dramatically in the cold night air beyond the yawning expanse of the Coosa Valley. Even when I am away from these mountains, bogged down in some city, caught up in the frenetic whirlpool of making a living, the mountains are inside me, just below the skin, in the blood.

For years I have tried unsuccessfully to abandon this peculiar need of mine for mountains, for high country and trout streams, for the economy of life that seems to follow a steady rise in altitude. It's a serious malady, a vexing obsession. Cure, remedies, anodynes?--I've tried my share. Sedatives to calm me down; syrups to soothe me; elixirs to steady me; even a therapy calling for the regular use of a poultice made from opossum-belly fur, beechnut paste, and a pinch of ginseng. The poultice was guaranteed to keep my mind out of the clouds and off rising trout. Like all the rest, it failed, miserably. I gave up on the poultice about three years ago. I was staying up at Fontana, North Carolina, and fishing Santeetlah Creek until I slipped, lost a fine brown trout, and decided to give the remedy up.

"What's the problem?" asked Erskine Lightman standing at the door of his two-room cabin down the mountain logging road from Santeetlah Creek near Robbinsville, North Carolina. He ran his long, heavily wrinkled hands through an imaginative crop of thick, unruly hair. Lightman is burdened with a curious array of eccentricities. Smoothing back the hair that isn't on his perfectly bald head is one of them. He turned his attention from his head to the old stove that occupies the middle of the cabin. Breakfast was on.

"It doesn't work," I said. Lightman swung the door wide, motioned me to come in, have a seat.

He walked to the stove, examined a pot of hot, sticky grits. A long moment of silence limped between us like a crippled specter.

Finally, he said, "Okay, you've got me. I'm curious. What in the hell doesn't work?!"

"The CURE!" I groaned, too upset to work up a good shout. I had spent the morning down on the creek above the bridge and lost a fine brown trout. I saw its shadow just before it wrapped the tippet section of my line around a stone and broke it off. I was thinking about that shadow, trying to project it against all the other piscine shadows that clutter my imagination. A fine trout. Another ghost to haul around in my head. Desperate for detail, for a look in its black eyes, I had lunged after the trout, a move that resulted in an acrobatic though momentary pirouette that quickly crumbled and left me chest-deep in the creek's cold rush of water. That's when I packed up my rod and reel, wrung out my socks and pants, and went looking for Erskine Lightman.

Small puddles of creek water gathered beneath my chair. Erskine sat down across from me and put a platter of grits between us, the grits looking like a detailed papier-mache model of the desolate, icebound peaks of The Himalayas.

"I don't have the mind I had a season ago," Erskine said as he went for the grits. "What is this cure supposed to cure, exactly?"

"Everything," I said. "All this mountain madness of mine. The endless pursuit of high country trout and my courtship of solitude. All of it." The words came somber and heavy, carried by breath that sounded like a gritty moan.

The smile was coming by then, though. I could see the corners of Erskine's mouth tremble as he fought back a loud burst of laughter.

"I thought you said heights make you dizzy, give you one hell of a case of vertigo. Just keep putting that poultice on your chest once a month and you can hang by your toes from the tallest building in Knoxville and still be steady as a preacher. Remember, though, rub it on you in ever smaller circles or it's worthless, and you'll panic climbing up a two-step staircase. And let's not hear any more about this genuine little twenty-five-dollar Smoky Mountain ointment not working."

I sneezed. "Okay, but what about my obsession with mountains and mountain streams and trout?" I asked, trying to dry out my bandanna by holding it near the woodstove.

This is what Erskine Lightman, fifth-generation master of Smoky Mountain folk medicine and trout fishing said, "Only one thing to do: shoot yourself."

And he couldn't hold the laughter anymore and we both let go at once and the morning was filled with it, a noise that seemed to rattle every board and nail of the old cabin. And I told Erskine about the brown trout again, which had already grown an inch in my memory, and beyond the front door you could see that sunlight was filling the narrow valley, a wall of light as wide and flat as a glacier inching inexorably toward the cabin door.

It's true about the poultice. Erskine prescribed it for a fever, which broke just as soon as I got out of my bed at home and drove up into the mountains and fished for a day along the bottom reaches of Hazel Creek. The only cure for a man in love with mountains is mountains; the analgesic for an addiction to mountain trout streams is the sound and feel of them--the low howling of water cascading over smooth stones; the sudden chill of a stream's mist against the skin; the knot in the gut and the adrenaline that spills into the blood on seeing a rising trout; that possibility of wildness that never dulls or wears thin, no matter the press of time, the passage of years.

. . . . With a fly rod, I can look foolish, be foolish, and still leap joyfully as a child into the heart of a fast-moving mountain river, into ranges that often seem as though they might reach beyond the dimmest stars. The fly rod not only catches trout; it is a handy fulcrum allowing me to cast to those things that seem so far beyond my grasp.

Of course, each new day also brings the sad prospect that I will leap and find that there is no firm ground under me. Mountains and mountain streams, like people, die, though usually for different reasons. They are ruined piecemeal, used to fuel what seems to be mankind's insatiable greed, the unappeased appetites of progress, development, prosperity. Man's economy, an economy of ever greater accumulation regardless of the price either to his kind or to the earth, seems to demand the destruction of the earth's natural economy. I am caught between the two, an angler seeking a compromise, a chance for man and the earth as well. I carry out my diplomacy in the mountains along trout streams. Mountains urge involvement. They urge motion, a searching not for the distant, but for what is near at hand. My leaps of faith are small matters and though I may cover no more ground than an atom, it's the leap that matters because it has measure and endurance, the force that might illuminate some truth sheltered in the sunlight, hidden in dark earth or twilight shadows. Such things are still possible even where wilderness, true wilderness, is but a distant relic of ancient time.

There is no true wilderness left in the Smoky Mountains. Wilderness must be free of man's taint and his history, and the presence of man marks these mountains well, has sculpted them as surely as has wind and water and every press of weather. These mountains are a latticework of life's scars, a quilt of struggle and defeat, independence, sadness, poverty, humor, and self-reliance, and starched faith. Even in the sad malaise of ruin, mountains are as pitiless as time itself.

The idea is not to fight mountains, but to absorb them. Off and on tonight I have been thinking of the sometimes difficult trail along Slickrock Creek up in the Joyce Kilmer Memorial Forest. The creek is beautiful, one of my favorite places in the mountains. Thinking of the hard trail, I find that concentration feeds on detail, on every remembered smell, every leaf in the wind, every tree remembered, until the image seems exact and sends a shiver under my skin and fills my blood with sizzling neuropeptides that put a reddish flush on my cheeks and neck, send something like a jolt of electricity through the muscles and nerves. Reality often seems to have a harder edge in the mountains, as though altitude somehow hones it, makes it spare, clean, raw, and honest--an addictive chaos of life that percolates through every atom.

Too often have I turned to the earth for some kind of dramatic statement. What is here is here and yet we search for the eccentric, the bizarre. We dissect and analyze, probe and examine, slide the earth under a microscope's lens hoping to find a code for miracles. Meanwhile, the sun shines and rivers rush and trout rise, and every hour of every day there is a real magic show of light and shadow and the dance of time. Nature is a grand balancing act, life in pursuit of a homeostasis it never quite achieves because its energy is always pushing it further on, tipping the balance, first one way, then the other.

Human beings come equipped with something called vestibular sensors, which are located in the inner ear. They give us a sense of balance, keep us level, if not level-headed. Mountains are vestibular sensors on a grander scale, absorbing the world about them, struggling for balance.

Down here, down on this Alabama hillside, it doesn't take much to upset the fragile disposition of my vestibular sensors. Traffic jams, bills to pay, love gone sour, a leaky roof, a truck with a whimsical starter, and, instantly, my sensors go haywire and I am as clumsy as a drunk haplessly trying to get up a down escalator. This is my body's way of telling me it is time to pack the fly rods and backpack and get back up into the mountains, back up along a good trout stream where I can enjoy the company of trout, which, for the most part, live far saner and more well-balanced lives.

There is a Beatles' song on the radio, music a church down the hillside tells me will get me to Hell a lot faster than I'm already going. I let the music play and recall the last time I heard the song up on Highway 441 driving from Tennessee to North Carolina and thinking that if I drove far enough, gained enough altitude, I would find a good run of water where I might have some say over what assaults my senses. The mountains never let me down. High among the clouds, the spectacular and the ordinary, the common and the exquisite, all take shape in the same light and disappear in the same common shadows. Ten steps on a narrow mountain trial and the heavy scales of urban life begin to fall away like so much dead skin and I become, almost unconsciously, the honest sum of my parts: a trout angler at loose ends, fishing from first light till last, filling my creel with so much more than trout.

This need for altitude, for cold mountain streams and the possibility of trout, is, I admit, getting more and more impulsive, harder to predict, harder to control. More and more, it surfaces without warning, leaving me happily bewildered and dazzled. One instant I'm putting an edge on a hoe and the next I am an empty sensorium, greedy for a trout stream's endless flood of stimuli, yearning for mountains laced with fall color, desperate for a hollow's rich smells, eager for the sight of a trout flashing just below the surface of the water. It's hard to relax. Every nerve seems a boisterous interpreter of what it feels. The message to the brain is plain, simple: time is not hard, not flat, one-dimensional. Rather, it is fluid, as dynamic and chaotic as a wild mountain river. I want to use it up as fully and completely as it uses me up, feed on it the way it feeds on me--mercilessly.

In the mountains experience is as rich in vital nutrition as chili and sourdough bread. Sometimes I have lived for days on the energy generated by experience. It is filling and satisfying and lingers in every cell. A scientist who keeps track of such things says that each second of our lives we are bombarded by at least 100,000 random impulses of sensory information. A holocaust of electrical information. Against such an onslaught I fumble about desperately like a man who has suddenly lost his sight and is trying to channel the earth--through one less sense.

The mountains dig at my senses, scrape them clean, wash them in cold mountain rivers, and hang them in a mountain wind to dry. Wading in a fine stream, I often try to reduce myself to a cell within its waters, nondescript flotsam riding wildly on the current of time as it spreads without fanfare down through shadow-filled, rocky valleys and finally onto the wide, flat, sunlit sprawl of the piedmont. I let such moments carry me for as long as they can and as far away as they can from that which seems to be doing me so little good--office politics and intrigue, neither of which I excel in, crowds, bad plumbing, polluted water and grimy air, traffic gridlock, the increasingly dreary task of simply making a living instead of living a life. Up in the mountains, I let all this go for a time and let myself drift toward what I like and enjoy rather than what others believe I need. Be it for an hour or a day or a week, when I am in the high country, I give up and give in, glide with slants of light, dream in cool shadows, cast my line after a good fish.

Parks Lanier
Writing About Literature

A man stands motionless in the water, a rod in his hand. Though we are too far away to see it, we know that from the end of the rod a very fine but strong filament extends into the water. At the end of the line, beneath the water, the real drama is taking place. The man is a motionless participant in that drama, but his mind is ceaselessly active as he considers what he is doing. Not only is he thinking about fishing, but he is also thinking about how he will behave once he catches a fish. And from moment to moment he tries to think like the fish he is trying to catch. "Where would I be if I were a trout on this beautiful day?" he considers.

When Ann Berthoff visited Radford University in April 1983, to conduct a session on Writing Across the Curriculum, she reminded us of one of I.A. Richards' most deeply held convictions, that the imagination is a speculative instrument, something to think *with* not just *about*. In writing about literature, one should approach the story or poem in the same way a fisherman approaches his trout. One should think *with* it, not merely *about* it.

The poem or story which you see printed on a page is itself a speculative instrument. It is the record of a mind in action. Before it was committed to paper, the work existed in the mind of the writer as pure action. Thus the poem or story, as you finally meet it, is an instrument to think *with*, not merely *about*. If you are accustomed to thinking of a piece of literature as something that has died on the page, like a fish out of water, or as something which has no life until you resuscitate it, then this essay will be nonsense to you. If, however, you know that a poem or story has a life of its own, and that you must live *with* it, then you will enjoy fishing with me.

Izaak Walton, author of *The Compleat Angler* (1653), says, ". . . angling is an art, and an art worth your learning. The question is . . . whether you be capable of learning it, for angling is somewhat like poetry; men are to be born so: I mean, with inclinations to it, though both may be heightened by discourse and practice: but he that hopes to be a good angler must not only bring an inquiring, searching, observing wit, but he must bring a large measure of hope and patience, and a love and propensity to the art itself. . . ."[1] The fisherman and the poet are much alike. But what of him who follows after the fisherman, the poet, and the storyteller?

The necessity or importance of writing about literature, that is, about something which has already been *written,* seems on the surface a bit absurd. The French philosopher Gaston Bachelard, however, reminds us that with a good book or a good poem we will read and re-read until we make a work ours and come to understand "*the problem* that confronted the author" until finally, imperceptibly, we give ourselves the illusion that both the problem and the solution are ours. The psychological nuance: 'I should have written that,' establishes us as phenomenologists of reading."[2] Writing about what we have read is one way of making it most completely our own, and, inevitably, in writing about literature we are writing about ourselves. The trick, however, is to make a mirror which is a lamp for the reader.

To help us understand the process of reading--and writing about--literature, Jeff Daniel Marion, a poet from Carson-Newman College in Tennessee, has written "Tight Lines," a poem which is about itself:

Tight Lines

1	First read the water,
2	then cast toward pockets,
3	the deep spaces between
4	the cold print of rocks.
5	It's the flow that beguiles--
6	what's beneath that lures.
7	But when the line goes
8	taut,
9	a dark, waiting presence
10	will flash
11	and weave its way,
12	throbbing, into your pulse.[3]

In only a dozen lines, Danny conveys not only what happens when we read a poem, but also what happens when we prepare to write about it.

In the course of his poem, Danny Marion discerns seven stages of a writer's response to a work of literature. First, there is the initial confrontation, which demands accuracy, honesty, and fidelity to what the work says (line 1). What is involved is an almost "scientific" scrupulousness. For example, if you title your essay "Jonah and the Whale," you obviously haven't read the water carefully enough. The text says that "a great fish" swallowed Jonah. Whales, as anyone who has read those tedious cetology chapters in *Moby Dick* knows, are mammals, not fish. Your title would make a scientific error.

"Poets and scientists have a lot in common," Ann Berthoff believes. "Scientists," she claims, "can discover the uses of syntax, the resources of language, by studying poetry." And she tells of how Yeats scholar T. R. Henn set scientists to studying the poetry of John Donne as a way of tuning their ears to the language. Would the resulting analysis or writing in any sense be "scientific"?

We who teach literary analysis--writing about literature--believe that it is a discipline which is not basically different from other types of analysis. Also, we believe that the concerns of careful literary analysis carry over into writing on other subjects. Indeed, there may be virtues of writing to be learned as part of literary analysis which will enrich other writing, virtues which cannot be learned elsewhere. For example, an entomologist who writes about Poe's "Sonnet: To Science" may later, in writing his scientific reports on creatures whose wings are "dull realities," discover how not to be dull himself--and in the process prove Poe's nasty little poem wrong. But the entomologist and the English major both must first "read the water," carefully and accurately.

What muddies the water so that it is unreadable? (1) The ego of the reader/writer. (2) Distractions external to the work, such as the biography of the poet or novelist. Those of us who spend our lives reading and trying to teach others how to read and say sensible (if not always profound) things about literature know that writing about literature has certain dangers. First of all, we recognize the subjectivity of the experience, and so we really don't want to write about the poem or story at all, but only about how "I" feel. Or we may have an author with a fascinating life, full of scandal and horrors of every kind, and so we'd rather write about his or her life, and make the literature an excuse for doing so. Or, and this is the worst danger of all, we really don't want to write about literature but about something else. Those who want to burn or ban books often fall into this third category.

Only after we have "read the water" clearly can we make the cognitive leap or, like the fisherman, cast a line with the expectation of catching something. We may cast several times before we are satisfied. Good writers and good fishermen are selective. We ask ourselves, "What approach to this poem or story is most productive? Shall it be extrinsic--biographical, psychological, social, philosophical, or comparative? Shall it be intrinsic--stylistic, metaphorical, or symbolic?" Here each writer is free to choose which "pocket" (line 2) to cast toward.

That decision having been made, the writer must realize that there are "deep spaces between/the cold print of rocks" (lines 3-4). That is, in approaching any work of literature one must be alert to distinguishing between what is *said* and what is *meant*. The unwary fisherman may discover that the water which seemed to his superficial glance only six inches deep is really six feet deep. And yet I am afraid that one of the worst charges laid against literature today, and against explications and essays on literature, is that it is all superficially deep (vide: *oxymoron*). Writing about literature is too often regarded as a kind of scavenger hunt for hidden meanings.

Danny Marion offers us a way out of all these suspicions and hostilities bound up with writing about literature. Ultimately, he says, "it's the flow that beguiles" (line 5). The good fisherman is attentive to the whole stream, not just his little fishin' hole. One who writes about literature must also have a sense of the *whole* and be alert to contextual relationships. Look back at Danny Marion's own poem. At what point does it begin to "flow" away from being just a poem about fishing to being a poem about our approach to literature? Within the context of the poem, how many different meanings does its title have? Why can it have more than one?

Gaston Bachelard says that as readers we want to understand "*the problem that confronted the author.*" Writers about literature usually express that as concern for an author's theme, or, as Danny Marion says, it's "what's beneath that lures" (line 6). The most difficult part of writing about literature is stating the abstract foundation (theme) upon which the work under analysis rises as a specific example. We would much rather write about Romeo or Juliet than cope with a theory of tragedy. But Danny Marion is right. Ultimately it is "what's beneath that lures" us and keeps us coming back again and again to a work of literature. It is what has made shelves of Shakespearian scholarship out of three dozen plays. Gaston Bachelard is right, too, in saying that "imperceptibly, we give ourselves the illusion that both the solution and the problem are ours." That, largely, is the reward we are expecting when we write about literature.

To attain that reward, however, the writer must have a "tight line." Part of what Danny Marion is describing in lines 7-8 of his poem is the formulation of a precise thesis for the literary analysis. Once the writer "knows" something about a poem or story that no one else knows, "the line goes/taut" (lines 7-8). He has caught something--or been caught. This moment is described by skilled fishermen as "setting the hook." The first paragraph of a paper usually does just that so the reader doesn't get away.

Danny Marion is keenly aware that the fisherman and his fish, the writer and his subject, and the writer and his audience all form one "tight line" of mutual interplay. At the moment of the tightening of the line, "a dark, waiting presence/will flash/and weave its way,/throbbing, into your pulse" (lines 9-12). Everyone who writes about literature realizes that the whole of the creative work under analysis will always be greater than the sum of its parts, that there is indeed a subjective emotional response which no objective analysis can ever perfectly articulate. No fisherman can ever tell the whole story of what the catch *really* was like. There is that "throbbing" pulse of excitement--the ultimate "tight line"--that can never be conveyed unless the reader is flesh of your flesh and pulse of your pulse. The writer who comes closest to doing that is the writer we love most and remember the longest. The writer who can show us the life that is in a poem or story earns our everlasting gratitude.

Notes

[1]Izaak Walton, *The Compleat Angler, 1653* (London: J. M. Dent and Company, 1899), p. 28.

[2]Gaston Bachelard, *The Poetics of Space*, trans. Maria Jolas (Boston: Beacon Press, 1958), p. 21.

[3]The poem "Tight Lines" gives its title to a collection of twenty-two poems by Jeff Daniel Marion, published in 1981 by Iron Mountain Press, Emory, Virginia. The poem also appears in the anthology *I Have a Place*, edited by Jim Wayne Miller, and in *New Ground*, edited by D. Askins and D. Morris. It appears here by special permission of the author, and may not be further used without his permission.

Guy L. Osborne
O, Appalachia: Artists of the Southern Mountains

An exhibition organized by the Huntington Museum of Art, Huntington, W.Va. On Tour May 1990 - February 1993.

In religion a half-truth presented as the whole truth is called heresy and its adherents are banished or burned at the stake. In art half-truths can be called "folk art" and exhibited without controversy as an expression of the essential experience and character of a particular people.

Such is the case in this exhibition of works by "artists of the southern mountains," which is on tour through eight states in the South and Midwest until 1993.

The exhibition consists of works by some 20 self-taught artists and craftmakers from West Virginia, Kentucky, Georgia, North Carolina, Tennessee, and Virginia, including paintings, sculptures, figurines, mixed media compositions, and handmade baskets, knives, plates, and bowls. Most are on loan from two private collections.

An interpretive brochure is provided for viewers, which purports to give a psychological account of the exhibit. The artists, we are told, have been molded by the "isolation" and "rugged nature" of their homeland to become "tenacious and self-reliant" with a "strong belief in nature, religion and selfworth." They are somehow endowed by their "mountain surroundings" to "respond naturally...by producing art...to translate their Appalachian experience for themselves and others." Their creativity springs, not from any training or exposure to traditional art forms, but from the very "spirit of Appalachia, a spirit that is as beautiful and indomitable as the Southern Mountains they call home."

A book, *O, Appalachia*, preceded the tour and contains photographs of many of the works in the exhibition. The book was reviewed in *AppalJ* by Woodrow Hill (Spring 1991) who was impressed by its visual quality and the eccentricity of the artists and their works. Although Hill probably makes several valid points from the perspective of art criticism, he seems not to recognize the limited and largely romanticized depictions of Appalachia present in both the book and in this exhibition.

Don't get me wrong; the exhibit is definitely worth seeing. Many individual works are imaginative, colorful renderings in wood or on canvas of interesting subjects. Many reflect powerful religious themes. The toyish figurines delight the eyes with their detail and humor. Several works, surreal depictions of death and evil in human life, evoke complex emotional and intellectual responses. The crafts are exquisite in their handiwork, which highlights the beauty of the natural materials used.

The problem with the exhibition is its incompleteness, its heresy if you will. Presented as a reflection of the "Appalachian experience," these works in fact represent a wide range of some experiences while ignoring other important possibilities, resulting in a exhibition which is more stereotypical than insightful in its treatment of mountain life and people.

For example, noticeably absent are any artistic expressions by Native Americans, or by artists from the region with any formal training whose work reflects their sense of place, or by songwriters and poets who have chronicled the stories of working people and their struggles with the economic exploitation and political domination during Appalachia's period of "colonization" by corporate interests.

The variety of experiences which is present in the exhibition deserves more recognition than it is given. There is a real range of artistic style and interest here. Some of the works are rather simple, spontaneous, and straightforward, even childlike. In contrast, several of the artists appear quite deliberate in their use of symbol and introspection dealing with universal themes which defy easy categorization as folk art. The crafts are a different genre altogether.

The failure to differentiate is a telling symptom that one culture is defining another by its own projections and limited understandings. The failure of this exhibition is not in the individual works but in the interpretation imposed upon them (not only by the viewer brochure but implicitly by the limited content chosen for display under a title as panoramic as *0, Appalachia*). These objects just do not form a coherent and complete story.

Whatever Appalachia is, it is not neatly contained in the limited array of art works and images selected for display. A visit to the new Whittle Communications building in Knoxville or to the migrant worker encampments in Cocke County, Tenn., will show you that. Whoever these people of Appalachia are, they are not merely eccentric mountain folk living off to themselves in harmony with nature and neighbor. A look at the activism and accomplishments of the likes of Ron Eller and John Gaventa and at the tragic rates of unemployment, school failure, and infant mortality in Campbell County, Tenn., will show you that. And whatever possesses human beings to express themselves artistically, intuition tells me it is a more complex thing than growing up in the hills. My guess is that poor and disfranchised people from the cities and the flatlands are just as driven to express themselves artistically.

This exhibition is an eclectic assortment of interesting works of arts and crafts by a rather small number of individuals from dispersed areas in the South who have many different things to say for what are undoubtedly many different reasons. As Woodrow Hill correctly observes, "The art of a few is Appalachian because that is where they have chosen to work."

In his recent book *Apples on the Flood*, which analyzes the historical, cultural, and psychological complexities of the Appalachian experience, Rodger Cunningham warns, "It is important not only to avoid blanket generalizations...but also to recognize the importance of factors such as social class, the distinction between rural and urban, and in modern times the necessity of defense against forces which, in addition to being socially and culturally destructive, are physically destructive to the land itself." Any art exhibition which purports to be of Appalachia would do well to heed this warning.

Wendell Berry
from *A Native Hill*

Pull down thy vanity, it is not man
Made courage, or made order, or made grace,
Pull down thy vanity, I say pull down.
Learn of the green world what can be thy place...
                    --Ezra Pound, Canto LXXXI

The hill is not a hill in the usual sense. It has no "other side." It is an arm of Kentucky's central upland known as The Bluegrass; one can think of it as a ridge reaching out from that center, progressively cut and divided, made ever narrower by the valleys of the creeks that drain it. The town of Port Royal in Henry County stands on one of the last heights of this upland, the valleys of two creeks, Gullion's Branch and Cane Run, opening on either side of it into the valley of the Kentucky River. My house backs against the hill's foot where it descends from the town to the river. The river, whose waters have carved the hill and so descended from it, lies within a hundred steps of my door.

Within about four miles of Port Royal, on the upland and in the bottoms upriver, all my grandparents and great-grandparents lived and left such memories as their descendants have bothered to keep. Little enough has been remembered. The family's life here goes back to my mother's great-great-grandfather and to my father's great-grandfather, but of those earliest ones there are only a few vague word-of-mouth recollections. The only place antecedent to this place that has any immediacy to any of us is the town of Cashel in County Tipperary, Ireland, which one of my great-grandfathers left as a boy to spend the rest of his life in Port Royal. His name was James Mathews, and he was a shoemaker. So well did he fit his life into this place that he is remembered, even in the family, as having belonged here. The family's only real memories of Cashel are my own, coming from a short visit I made there five years ago.

And so such history as my family has is the history of its life here. All that any of us may know of ourselves is to be known in relation to this place. And since I did most of my growing up here, and have had most of my most meaningful experiences here, the place and the history, for me, have been inseparable, and there is a sense in which my own life is inseparable, and I have been both enriched and bewildered by it.

———————

Sometimes I can no longer think in the house or in the cleared fields. They bear too much resemblance to our failed human history--failed, because it has led to this human present that is such a bitterness and a trial. And so I go to the woods. As I go under the trees, dependable, almost at once, and by nothing I do, things fall into place. I enter an order that does not exist outside, in human spaces. I feel my life take its place among the lives--the trees, the annual plants, the animals and birds, the living of all these and the dead--that go and have gone to make the life of the earth. I am less important than I thought, the human race is less important than I thought. I rejoice in that. My mind loses its urgings, senses its nature, and is free. The forest grew here in its own time, and so I will live, suffer and rejoice, and die in my own time. There is nothing that I may decently hope for that I cannot reach by patience as well as by anxiety. The hill, which is a part of America, has killed no one in the service of the American government. Then why should I, who am a fragment of the hill? I wish to be as peaceable as my land, which does no violence, though it has been the scene of violence and has had violence done to it.

How, having a consciousness, and intelligence, a human spirit--all the vaunted equipment of my race--can I humble myself before a mere piece of the earth and speak of myself as its fragment? Because my mind transcends the hill only to be filled with it, to comprehend it a little, to know that it lives on the hill in time as well as in place, to recognize itself as the hill's fragment.

The false and truly belittling transcendence is ownership. The hill has had more owners than its owners have had years--they are grist for its mill. It has had few friends well. It tells them they are fragments of its life. In its life they transcend their years.

———————

The most exemplary nature is that of the topsoil. It is very Christ-like in its passivity and beneficence, and in the penetrating energy that issues out of its peaceableness. It increases by experience, by the passage of seasons over it, growth rising out of it and returning to it, not by ambition or aggressiveness. It is enriched by all things that die and enter into it. It keeps the past, not as history or as memory, but as richness, new possibility. Its fertility is always building up out of death into promise. Death is the bridge or the tunnel by which its past enters its future.

To walk in the woods, mindful only of the physical extent of it, is to go perhaps as owner, or as knower, confident of one's own history and of one's own importance. But to go there, mindful as well of its temporal extent, of the age of it, and of all that led up to the present life of it, and of all that may follow it, is to feel oneself a flea in the pelt of a great living thing, the discrepancy between its life and one's own so great that it cannot be imagined. One has come into the presence of mystery. After all the trouble one has taken to be a modern man, one has come back under the spell of a primitive awe, wordless and humble.

Wendell Berry
In This World

The hill pasture, an open place among the trees,
tilts into the valley. The clovers and tall grasses
are in bloom. Along the foot of the hill
dark floodwater moves down the river.
The sun sets. Ahead of nightfall the birds sing.
I have climbed up to water the horses
and now sit and rest, high on the hillside,
letting the day gather and pass. Below me
cattle graze out across the wide fields of the bottomlands,
slow and preoccupied as stars. In this world
men are making plans, wearing themselves out,
spending their lives, in order to kill each other.

Wendell Berry
A Standing Ground

However just and anxious I have been,
I will stop and step back
from the crowd of those who may agree
with what I say, and be apart.
There is no earthly promise of life or peace
but where the roots branch and weave
their patient silent passages in the dark;
uprooted, I have been furious without an aim.
I am not bound for any public place,
but for ground of my own
where I have planted vines and orchard trees,
and in the heat of the day climbed up
into the healing shadow of the woods.
Better than any argument is to rise at dawn
and pick dew-wet berries in a cup.

Wendell Berry
The Peace of Wild Things

When despair for the world grows in me
and I wake in the night at the least sound
in fear of what my life and my children's lives may be,
I go and lie down where the wood drake
rests in his beauty on the water, and the great heron
feeds. I come into the peace of wild things
who do not tax their lives with forethought
of grief. I come into the presence of still water.
And I feel above me the day-blind stars
waiting with their light. For a time
I rest in the grace of the world, and am free.

Wendell Berry
To Know the Dark

To go in the dark with a light is to know the light.
To know the dark, go dark. Go without sight,
and find that the dark, too, blooms and sings,
and is traveled by dark feet and dark wings.

Lynn Powell
The Calling

But lay up for yourselves treasures in heaven,
where neither moth nor rust doth corrupt...
                                        --Matthew 6:20

Retired missionaries taught us Arts and Crafts
each July at Bible Camp:
how to glue the kidney, navy, and pinto
bean into mosaics, and how to tool the stenciled
butterfly on copper sheets they'd cut for us.
At night, after hymns, they'd cut the lights and show us slides:
wide-spread trees, studded with corsage;
saved women tucking T-shirts into wrap-around batiks;
a thatched church whitewashed in the equator's light.
Above the hum of the projector I could hear the insects flick
their heads against the windowscreens, aiming
for the brightness of that Africa.

If Jesus knocks on your heart, be ready to say,
'Send me, O Lord, send me,' a teacher told us
confidentially, dolling out her baggies of dried corn.
I bent my head, concentrating hard on my tweezers
as I glued each colored kernel into a rooster
for Mother's kitchen wall.

But Jesus noticed me and started to knock.
Already saved, I looked for signs to show me
what else he would require.
Rest hour, I closed my eyes and flipped my Bible open, slid
my finger, ouija-like, down the page, and there
was his command:
Go and do ye likewise--
Let the earth and all it contains hear--
Every tree that does not bear good fruit is cut
down and thrown into the fire--.

Thursday night, at revival service, I held out
through *Trust and Obey, Standing*
on the Promises, Nothing But the Blood, but
crumpled on *Softly and Tenderly*
Jesus is Calling, promising God, cross
my heart, I'd witness to Rhodesia.
Down the makeshift aisle I walked with the other
weeping girls and stood before the little
bit of congregation left singing
in their metal chairs.

The bathhouse that night was silent,
young Baptists moving from shower to sink
with the stricken look of nuns.
Inside a stall, I stripped, slipped my clothes outside
the curtain, and turned for the faucet--but there,
splayed on the shower's wall, was a luna moth,
the eyes of its wings fixed on me.
It shimmered against the cement block:
sherbert-green, plumed, a flamboyant verse
lodged in a page of drab ink.

I waved my hands to scare it out, but, blinkless,
it stayed latched on. Slowly
I moved so close only my breath
moved, stroking the fur on its animal back.

One by one the showers cranked dry.
The bathhouse door slammed a final time.
I pulled my clothes back over my sweat, drew
the curtain shut, and walked into a dark
pricked by the lightning bugs' inscrutable morse.

William L. Blevins
Stories, Myths, and Personal Identity

If storytelling is an art form, and I believe it is, my grandfather was an artist. From my earliest memories, I recall him telling stories. Sometimes he'd spin a yarn of his own creation as a teaser for my imagination. But most of the time his stories were true, verbal snapshots of his own life and experiences. Sometimes he'd retell a particular story, especially as he got older. Yet I never tired of hearing any of them. Even as an adult, I always turned my ears in his direction when he began a story.

My grandfather's repertoire of stories covered a wide variety of subjects. The one he told the most often concerned the New Market train wreck, a nineteenth-century accident preserved in folklore and folk music. Papa, that's what every one of my generation affectionately called him, was a teenager living in New Market, Tennessee at the time. He was plowing a field when he heard the noise of two trains colliding several miles away. A short time later, a neighbor dashed into the field and asked if he would go to the wreck site and search for her son, who was supposed to be on one of the trains. For several hours my grandfather helped injured victims as he searched for the young man among traumatized survivors and twisted pieces of iron. The neighbor's son, however, was nowhere to be found. As luck would have it, he'd missed the train in Knoxville and was sitting in the train station when the wreck occurred.

As a child, I thought the New Market train wreck story was merely an interesting historical reminiscence. Yet, later in life I realized that it was much more than that. The New Market story contained a hidden message about how Murrins are expected to behave in a crisis.

Other stories that I remember had to do with bricks that Papa helped to make--bricks that were used in the original Henderson Hall at Carson-Newman College. I have a few of those bricks at my house. They are now prized archaeological artifacts which provide a tangible link to my personal history. Also, there were stories about his playing baseball at C-N at the turn of the century, and what life was like when he was just a kid, and what went on when my mother was a little girl, and about fishing with his great-grandfather who was alive when George Washington was president. On the Murrin side of our family, that great-grandfather is called "the old man." Papa had a story for almost any situation. After he retired, he spent the winters in Florida. That practice converted into more stories--about rattle snakes, alligators, rabbits, oranges, and a colorful elderly gentleman who told Papa that he traveled by telephone.

During his life, I thought my grandfather's stories were simply that--just stories. But now I know differently. Storytelling is an ancient art that enables us to know about ourselves and our families. Without the oral tradition passed down in our particular clan, we'd have no family or personal identity.

Every family has a cache of stories, unique to the family, which are passed verbally from grandparent to parent to child across the generations. Why is it that some family stories are passed on and others are not? Why do families remember some events and forget others? Family stories survive because they are encoded with family values, ideals, expectations, and beliefs. Although the stories may not openly espouse these components, they still function as family myths, guiding and informing family members on how to live according to their particular family traditions.

Your family's stories reveal who you are and how you are expected to live. They identify family heroes and villians, as well as family values and expectation. The stories describe what is acceptable behavior and what is taboo. They preserve a body of family history which enables you to identify yourself within the family system. I believe this is true to such an extent that the process of knowing who you are is an impossible task without the context of your generational heritage. To know what it means to be an American, you must know something about your national history. In the same way, to know yourself, you must know your personal history. This history, in part, is embedded in the stories passed across the generations of your family.

If you have storytellers in your family, listen to the yarns they spin. There's more to what they say than meets the ear. Their stories comprise your personal mythology and are as important for your own life as are classical myths in every culture.

Section II

A Sense of Place
in Nature and the Community

Barbara Kingsolver
Homeland and Other Stories

Homeland

I

My great-grandmother belonged to the Bird Clan. Hers was one of the fugitive bands of Cherokee who resisted capture in the year that General Winfield Scott was in charge of prodding the forest people from their beds and removing them westward. Those few who escaped his notice moved like wildcat families through the Carolina mountains, leaving the ferns unbroken where they passed, eating wild grapes and chestnuts, drinking when they found streams. The ones who could not travel, the aged and the infirm and the very young, were hidden in deep cane thickets where they would remain undiscovered until they were bones. When the people's hearts could not bear any more, they laid their deerskin packs on the ground and settled again.

General Scott had moved on to other endeavors by this time, and he allowed them to thrive or perish as they would. They built clay houses with thin, bent poles for spines, and in autumn they went down to the streams where the sycamore trees had let their year's work fall, the water steeped brown as leaf tea, and the people cleansed themselves of the sins of the scattered-bone time. They called their refugee years The Time When We Were Not, and they were forgiven, because they had carried the truth of themselves in a sheltered place inside the flesh, exactly the way a fruit that has gone soft still carries inside itself the clean, hard stone of its future.

II

My name is Gloria St. Clair, but like most people I've been called many things. My maiden name was Murray. My grown children have at one time or another hailed me by nearly anything pronounceable. When I was a child myself, my great-grandmother called me by the odd name of Waterbug. I asked her many times why this was, until she said once, to quiet me, "I'll tell you that story."

We were on the front-porch swing, in summer, in darkness. I waited while she drew tobacco smoke in and out of her mouth, but she said nothing. "Well," I said.

Moonlight caught the fronts of her steel-framed spectacles and she looked at me from her invisible place in the dark. "I said I'd tell you that story. I didn't say I would tell it right now."

We lived in Morning Glory, a coal town hacked with sharp blades out of a forest that threatened always to take it back. The hickories encroached on the town, springing up unbidden in the middle of dog pens and front yards and the cemetery. The creeping vines for which the town was named drew themselves along wire fences and up the sides of houses with the persistence of the displaced. I have heard it said that if a man stood still in Morning Glory, he would be tied down by vines and not found until first frost. Even the earth underneath us sometimes moved to repossess its losses: the long, deep shafts that men opened to rob the coal veins would close themselves up again, as quietly as flesh wounds.

My great-grandmother lived with us for her last two years. When she came to us we were instructed to call her Great Grandmother, but that proved impossible and so we called her Great Mam. My knowledge of her life follows an oddly obscured pattern, like a mountain road where much of the scenery is blocked by high laurel bushes, not because they were planted there, but because no one thought to cut them down.

I know that her maternal lineage was distinguished. Her mother's mother's father was said to have gone to England, where he dined with King George and contracted smallpox. When he returned home his family plunged him into an icy stream, which was the curative custom, and he died. Also, her mother was one of the Bird Clan's Beloved Women. When I asked what made her a Beloved Woman, Great Mam said that it was because she kept track of things.

But of Great Mam's own life, before she came to us, I know only a little. She rarely spoke of personal things, favoring instead the legendary and the historic, and so what I did discover came from my mother, who exercised over all matters a form of reverse censorship: she spoke loudly and often of events of which she disapproved, and rarely of those that might have been ordinary or redemptive. She told us, for instance, that Great-Grandfather Murray brought Great Mam from her tribal home in the Hiwassee Valley to live in Kentucky, without Christian sanction, as his common-law wife. According to Mother, he accomplished all of this on a stolen horse. From that time forward Great Mam went by the name of Ruth.

It was my mother's opinion that Great-Grandfather Murray was unfit for respectable work. He died after taking up the honest vocation of coal mining, which also killed their four sons, all on the same day, in a collapsed shaft. Their daughter perished of fever after producing a single illegitimate boy, who turned out to be my father, John Murray. Great Mam was thus returned to refugee ways, raising her grandson alone in hard circumstances, moving from place to place where she could find the odd bit of work. She was quite remarkably old when she came to us.

I know, also, that her true name was Green Leaf, although there is no earthly record of this. The gravesite is marked Ruth. Mother felt we ought to bury her under her Christian name in the hope that God in His infinite mercy would forget about the heathen marriage and stolen horses and call her home. It is likely, however, that He might have passed over the headstone altogether in his search for her, since virtually all the information written there is counterfeit. We even had to invent a date and year of birth for her since these things were unknown. This, especially, was unthinkable to my brothers and me. But we were children, of course, and believed our own birthdays began and ended the calendar.

To look at her, you would not have thought her an Indian. She wore blue and lavender flowered dresses with hand-tatted collars, and brown lace-up shoes with sturdy high heels, and she smoked a regular pipe. She was tall, with bowed calves and a faintly bent-forward posture, spine straight and elbows out and palms forward, giving the impression that she was at any moment prepared to stoop and lift a burden of great bulk or weight. She spoke with a soft hill accent, and spoke properly. My great-grandfather had been an educated man, more prone in his lifetime to errors of judgment than errors of grammar.

Great Mam smoked her pipe mainly in the evenings, and always on the front porch. For a time I believed this was because my mother so vigorously objected to the smell, but Great Mam told me otherwise. A pipe had to be smoked outdoors, she said, where the smoke could return to the Beloved Old Father who gave us tobacco. When I asked her what she meant, she said she meant nothing special at all. It was just the simplest thing, like a bread-and-butter note you send to an aunt after she has fed you a meal.

I often sat with Great Mam in the evenings on our porch swing, which was suspended by four thin, painted chains that squeaked. The air at night smelled of oil and dust, and faintly of livestock, for the man at the end of our lane kept hogs. Great Mam would strike a match and suck the flame into her pipe, lighting her creased face in brief orange bursts.

"The small people are not very bright tonight," she would say, meaning the stars. She held surprising convictions, such as that in the daytime the small people walked among us. I could not begin to picture it.

"You mean down here in the world, or do you mean right here in Morning Glory?" I asked repeatedly. "Would they walk along with Jack and Nathan and me to school?"

She nodded. "They would."

"But why would they come *here*?" I asked.

"Well, why wouldn't they?" she said.

I thought about this for a while, entirely unconvinced.

"You don't ever have to be lonesome," she said. "That's one thing you never need be."

"But mightn't I step on one of them, if it got in my way and I didn't see it?"

Great Mam said, "No. They aren't that small."

She had particular names for many things, including the months. February she called "Hungry Month." She spoke of certain animals as if they were relatives our parents had neglected to tell us about. The cowering white dog that begged at our kitchen door she called "the sad little cousin." If she felt like it, on these evenings, she would tell me stories about the animals, their personalities and kindnesses and trickery, and the permanent physical marking they invariably earned by doing something they ought not to have done. "Remember that story," she often commanded at the end, and I would be stunned with guilt because my mind had wandered onto crickets and pencil erasers and Black Beauty.

"I might not remember," I told her. "It's too hard."

Great Mam allowed that I might *think* I had forgotten. "But you haven't. You'll keep it stored away," she said. "If it's important, your heart remembers."

I had known that hearts could break and sometimes even be attacked, with disastrous result, but I had not heard of hearts remembering. I was eleven years old. I did not trust any of my internal parts with the capacity of memory.

———————

When the seasons changed, it never occurred to us to think to ourselves, "This will be Great Mam's last spring. Her last June apples. Her last fresh roasting ears from the garden." She was like an old pine, whose accumulated years cause one to ponder how long it has stood, not how soon it will fall. Of all of us, I think Papa was the only one who believed she could die. He planned the trip to Tennessee. We children simply thought it was a great lark.

This was June, following a bad spring during which the whole southern spine of the Appalachians had broken out in a rash of wildcat strikes. Papa was back to work at last, no longer home taking up kitchen-table space, but still Mother complained of having to make soup of neckbones and cut our school shoes open to bare our too-long toes to summer's dust, for the whole darn town to see. Papa pointed out that the whole darn town had been on the picket lines, and wouldn't pass judgment on the Murray kids if they ran their bare bottoms down Main Street. And what's more, he said, it wasn't his fault if John L. Lewis had sold him down the river.

My brothers and I thrilled to imagine ourselves racing naked past the Post Office and the women shopping at Herman Ritchie's market, but we did not laugh out loud. We didn't know exactly who Mr. John L. Lewis was, or what river Papa meant, but we knew not to expect much. The last thing we expected was a trip.

My brother Jack, because of his nature and superior age, was suspicious from the outset. While Papa explained his plan, Jack made a point of pushing lima beans around his plate in single file to illustrate his boredom. It was 1955. Patti Page and Elvis were on the radio and high school boys were fighting their mothers over ducktails. Jack had a year to go before high school, but already the future was plainly evident.

He asked where in Tennessee we would be going, if we did go. The three of us had not seen the far side of a county line.

"The Hiwassee Valley, where Great Mam was born," Papa said.

My brother Nathan grew interested when Jack laid down his fork. Nathan was only eight, but he watched grownups. If there were no men around, he watched Jack.

"Eat your beans, Jack," Mother said. "I didn't put up these limas last fall so you could torment them."

Jack stated, "I'm not eating no beans with guts in them."

Mother took a swat at Jack's arm. "Young man, you watch your mouth. That's the insides of a hog, and a hog's a perfectly respectable animal to eat." Nathan was making noises with his throat. I tried not to make any face one way or the other.

Great Mam told Mother it would have been enough just to have the limas, without the meat. "A person can live on green corn and beans, Florence Ann," she said. "There's no shame in vegetables."

We knew what would happen next, and watched with interest. "If I have to go out myself and throw a rock at a songbird," Mother said, having deepened to the color of beetroot, "nobody is going to say this family goes without meat!"

Mother was a tiny woman who wore stockings and shirtwaists even to hoe the garden. She had yellow hair pinned in a tight bun, with curly bangs in front. We waited with our chins cupped in our palms for Papa's opinion of her plan to make a soup of Robin Redbreast, but he got up from the table and rummaged in the bureau drawer for the gas-station map. Great Mam ate her beans in a careful way, as though each one had its own private importance.

"Are we going to see Injuns?" Nathan asked, but on one answered. Mother began making a great deal of noise clearing up the dishes. We could hear her out in the kitchen, scrubbing.

Papa unfolded the Texaco map on the table and found where Tennessee and North Carolina and Georgia came together in three different pastel colors. Great Mam looked down at the colored lines and squinted, holding the sides of her glasses. "Is this the Hiwassee River?" she wanted to know.

"No, now those lines are highways," he said. "Red is interstate. Blue is river."

"Well, what's this?"

He looked. "That's the state line."

"Now why would they put that on the map? You can't see it."

Papa flattened the creases of the map with his broad hands, which were crisscrossed with fine black lines of coal dust, like a map themselves, no matter how clean. "The Hiwassee Valley's got a town in it now, it says 'Cherokee.' Right here."

"Well, those lines make my eyes smart," Great Mam said. "I'm not going to look anymore."

The boys started to snicker, but Papa gave us a look that said he meant business and sent us off to bed before it went any farther.

"Great Mam's blind as a post hole," Jack said once we were in bed. "She don't know a road from a river."

"She don't know beans from taters," said Nathan.

"You boys hush up, I'm tired," I said. Jack and Nathan slept lengthwise in the bed, and I slept across the top with my own blanket.

"Here's Great Mam," Nathan said. He sucked in his cheeks and crossed his eyes and keeled over backward, bouncing us all on the bedsprings. Jack punched him in the ribs, and Nathan started to cry louder then he had to. I got up and sat by the bedroom door hugging my knees, listening to Papa and Mother. I could hear them in the kitchen.

"As if I hadn't put up with enough, John. It's not enough that Murrays have populated God's earth without the benefit of marriage," Mother said. This was her usual starting point. She was legally married to my father in a Baptist Church, a fact she could work into any conversation.

"Well, I don't see why," she said, "if we never had the money to take the kids anyplace before."

Papa's voice was quieter, and I couldn't hear his answers.

"Was this her idea, John, or yours?"

When Nathan and Jack were asleep I went to the window and slipped over the sill. My feet landed where they always did, in the cool mud of Mother's gladiolus patch alongside the house. Great Mam did not believe in flower patches. Why take a hoe and kill all the growing things in a piece of ground, and then plant others that have been uprooted from somewhere else? This was what she asked me. She thought Mother spent a fearful amount of time moving things needlessly from one place to another.

"I see you, Waterbug," said Great Mam in the darkness, though what she probably meant was that she heard me. All I could see was the glow of her pipe bowl moving above the porch swing.

"Tell me the waterbug story tonight," I said, settling onto the swing. The fireflies were blinking on and off in the black air above the front yard.

"No, I won't," she said. The orange glow moved to her lap, and faded from bright to dim. "I'll tell you another time."

The swing squeaked its sad song, and I thought about Tennessee. It had never occurred to me that the place where Great Mam had been a child was still on this earth. "Why'd you go away from home?" I asked her.

"You have to marry outside your clan," she said. "That's law. And all the people we knew were Bird Clan. All the others were gone. So when Stewart Murray came and made baby eyes at me, I had to go with him." She laughed. "I liked his horse."

I imagined the two of them on a frisking, strong horse, crossing the mountains to Kentucky. Great Mam with black hair. "Weren't you afraid to go?" I asked.

"Oh, yes I was. The canebrakes were high as a house. I was afraid we'd get lost."

We were to leave on Saturday after Papa got off work. He worked days then, after many graveyard-shift years during which we rarely saw him except asleep, snoring and waking throughout the afternoon, with Mother forever forced to shush us; it was too easy to forget someone was trying to sleep in daylight. My father was a soft-spoken man who sometimes drank but was never mean. He had thick black hair, no beard stubble at all nor hair on his chest, and a nose he called his Cherokee nose. Mother said she thanked the Lord that at least He had seen fit not to put that nose on her children. She also claimed he wore his hair long to flout her, although it wasn't truly long, in our opinion. His nickname in the mine was "Indian John."

There wasn't much to get ready for the trip. All we had to do in the morning was wait for afternoon. Mother was in the house scrubbing so it would be clean when we came back. The primary business of Mother's life was scrubbing things, and she herself looked scrubbed. Her skin was the color of a clean boiled potato. We didn't get in her way.

My brothers were playing a ferocious game of cowboys and Indians in the backyard, but I soon defected to my own amusements along the yard's weedy borders, picking morning glories, pretending to be a June bride. I grew tired of trying to weave the flowers into my coarse hair and decided to give them to Great Mam. I went around to the front and came up the three porch steps in one jump, just exactly the way Mother said a lady wouldn't do.

"Surprise," I announced. "These are for you." The flowers were already wilting in my hand.

"You shouldn't have picked those," she said.

"They were a present." I sat down, feeling stung.

"Those are not mine to have and not yours to pick," she said, looking at me, not with anger but with intensity. Her brown pupils were as dark as two pits in the earth. "A flower is alive, just as much as you are. A flower is your cousin. Didn't you know that?"

I said, No ma'am, that I didn't.

"Well, I'm telling you now, so you will know. Sometimes a person has got to take a life, like a chicken's or a hog's when you need it. If you're hungry, then they're happy to give their flesh up to you because they're your relatives. But nobody is so hungry they need to kill a flower."

I said nothing.

"They ought to be left where they stand, Waterbug. You need to leave them for the small people to see. When they die they'll fall where they are, and make a seed for next year."

"Nobody cared about these," I contended. "They weren't but just weeds."

"It doesn't matter what they were or were not. It's a bad thing to take for yourself something beautiful that belongs to everybody. Do you understand? To take it is a sin."

I didn't, and I did. I could sense something of wasted life in the sticky leaves, translucent with death, and the purple flowers turning wrinkled and limp. I'd once brought home a balloon from a Ritchie child's birthday party, and it had shriveled and shrunk with just such a slow blue agony.

"I'm sorry," I said.

"It's all right." She patted my hands. "Just throw them over the porch rail there, give them back to the ground. The small people will come and take them back."

I threw the flowers over the railing in a clump, and came back, trying to rub the purple and green juices off my hands onto my dress. In my mothers's eyes, this would have been the first sin of my afternoon. I understood the difference between Great Mam's rules and the Sunday-school variety, and that you could read Mother's Bible forward and backward and never find where it said it's a sin to pick flowers because they are our cousins.

"I'll try to remember," I said.

"I want you to," said Great Mam. "I want you to tell your children."

"I'm not going to have any children," I said. "No boy's going to marry me. I'm too tall. I've got knob knees."

"Don't ever say you hate what you are." She tucked a loose sheaf of black hair behind my ear. "It's an unkindness to those that made you. That's like a red flower saying it's too red, do you see what I mean?"

"I guess," I said.

"You will have children. And you'll remember about the flowers," she said, and I felt the weight of these promises fall like a deerskin pack between my shoulder blades.

———————

By four o'clock we were waiting so hard we heard the truck crackle up the gravel road. Papa's truck was a rust-colored Ford with complicated cracks hanging like spiderwebs in the corners of the windshield. He jumped out with his long, blue-jean strides and patted the round front fender.

"Old Paint's had her oats," he said. "She's raring to go." This was a game he played with Great Mam. Sometimes she would say, "John Murray, you couldn't ride a mule with a saddle on it," and she'd laugh, and we would for a moment see the woman who raised Papa. Her bewilderment and pleasure, to have ended up with this broad-shouldered boy.

Today she said nothing, and papa went for Mother. There was only room for three in the cab, so Jack and Nathan and I climbed into the back with the old quilt Mother gave us and a tarpaulin in case of rain.

"What's she waiting for, her own funeral?" Jack asked me.

I looked at Great Mam, sitting still on the porch like a funny old doll. The whole house was crooked, the stoop sagged almost to the ground, and there sat Great Mam as straight as a schoolteacher's ruler. Seeing her there, I fiercely wished to defend my feeling that I knew her better than others did.

"She doesn't want to go," I said. I knew as soon as I'd spoken that it was the absolute truth.

"That's stupid. She's the whole reason we're going. Why wouldn't she want to go see her people?"

"I don't know, Jack," I said.

Papa and Mother eventually came out of the house, Papa in a clean shirt already darkening under the arms, and Mother with her Sunday purse, the scuff marks freshly covered with white shoe polish. She came down the front steps in the bent-over way she walked when she wore high heels. Papa put his hand under Great Mam's elbow and she silently climbed into the cab.

When he came around to the other side I asked him, "Are you sure Great Mam wants to go?"

"Sure she does," he said. "She wants to see the place where she grew up. Like what Morning Glory is to you."

"When I grow up I'm not never coming back to Morning Glory," Jack said.

"Me neither." Nathan spat over the side of the truck, the way he'd seen men do.

"Don't spit, Nathan," Papa said.

"Shut up," Nathan said, after Papa had gotten in the truck and shut the door.

The houses we passed had peeled paint and slumped porches like our own, and they all wore coats of morning-glory vines, deliciously textured and fat as fur coats. We pointed out to each other the company men's houses, which had bright white paint and were known to have indoor bathrooms. The deep ditches along the road, filled with blackberry brambles and early goldenrod, ran past us like rivers. On our walks to school we put these ditches to daily use practicing Duck and Cover, which was what our teachers felt we ought to do when the Communists dropped the H-bomb.

"We'll see Indians in Tennessee," Jack said. I knew we would. Great Mam had told me how it was.

"Great Mam don't look like an Indian," Nathan said.

"Shut up, Nathan," Jack said. "How do you know what an Indian looks like? You ever seen one?"

"She does so look like an Indian," I informed my brothers. "She is one."

According to Papa we all looked like little Indians, I especially. Mother hounded me continually to stay out of the sun, but by each summer's end I was so dark-skinned my schoolmates teased me, saying I ought to be sent over to the Negro school.

"Are we going to be Indians when we grow up?" Nathan asked.

"No, stupid," said Jack. "We'll just be same as we are now."

We soon ran out of anything productive to do. We played White Horse Zit many times over, until Nathan won, and we tried to play Alphabet but there weren't enough signs. The only public evidence of literacy in that part of the country was the Beech Nut Tobacco signs on barn roofs, and every so often, nailed to a tree trunk, a clapboard on which someone had painted "PREPARE TO MEET GOD."

Papa's old truck didn't go as fast as other cars. Jack and Nathan slapped the fenders like jockeys as we were passed on the uphill slopes, but their coaxing amounted to nought. By the time we went over Jellico Mountain, it was dark.

An enormous amount of sky glittered down at us on the mountain pass, and even though it was June we were cold. Nathan had taken the quilt for himself and gone to sleep. Jack said he ought to punch him one to teach him to be nice, but truthfully, nothing in this world could have taught Nathan to share. Jack and I huddled together under the tarp, which stank of coal oil, and sat against the back of the cab where the engine rendered up through the truck's metal body a faint warmth.

"Jack?" I said.

"What."

"Do you reckon Great Mam's asleep?"

He turned around and cupped his hands to see into the cab. "Nope," he said. "She's sitting up there in between 'em, stiff as a broom handle."

"I'm worried about her," I said.

"Why? If we were home she'd be sitting up just the same, only out front on the porch."

"I know."

"Glorie, you know what?" he asked me.

"What?"

A trailer truck loomed up behind us, decked with rows of red and amber lights like a Christmas tree. We could see the driver inside the cab. A faint blue light on his face made him seem ghostly and entirely alone. He passed us by, staring ahead, as though only he were real on this cold night and we were among all the many things that were not. I shivered, and felt an identical chill run across Jack's shoulders.

"What?" I asked again.

"What, what?"

"You were going to tell me something."

"Oh. I forgot what it was."

"Great Mam says the way to remember something you forgot is to turn your back on it. Say, 'The small people came dancing. They ran through the woods today.' Talk about what they did, and then whatever it was you forgot, they'll bring it back to you."

"That's dumb," Jack said. "That's Great Mam's hobbledy-gobbledy."

For a while we played See Who Can Go to Sleep First, which we knew to be a game that can't consciously be won. He never remembered what he'd meant to say.

———————

When Papa woke us the next morning we were at a truck stop in Knoxville. He took a nap in the truck with his boots sticking out the door while the rest of us went in for breakfast. Inside the restaurant was a long glass counter containing packs of Kools and Mars Bars lined up on cotton batting, objects of great value to be protected from dust and children. The waitress who brought us our eggs had a red wig perched like a bird on her head, and red eyebrows painted on over the real ones.

When it was time to get back in the truck we dragged and pulled on Mother's tired, bread-dough arms, like little babies, asking her how much farther.

"Oh, it's not far. I expect we'll be in Cherokee by lunchtime," she said, but her mouth was set and we knew she was as tired of this trip as any of us.

It was high noon before we saw a sign that indicated we were approaching Cherokee. Jack pummeled the cab window with his fists to make sure they all saw it, but Papa and Mother were absorbed in some kind of argument. There were more signs after that, with pictures of cartoon Indian boys urging us to buy souvenirs or stay in so-and-so's motor lodge. The signs were shaped like log cabins and teepees. Then we saw a real teepee. It was made of aluminum and taller than a house. Inside, it was a souvenir store.

We drove around the streets of Cherokee and saw that the town was all the same, as single-minded in its offerings as a corn patch or an orchard, so that it made no difference where we stopped. We parked in front of Sitting Bull's Genuine Indian Made Souvenirs, and Mother crossed the street to get groceries for our lunch. I had a sense of something gone badly wrong, like a lie told in my past and then forgotten, and now about to catch up with me.

A man in a feather war bonnet danced across from us in the parking lot. His outfit was a bright orange, with white fringe trembling along the seams of the pants and sleeves, and a woman in the same clothes sat cross-legged on the pavement playing a tom-tom while he danced. People with cameras gathered and side-stepped around one another to snap their shots. The woman told them that she and her husband Chief Many Feathers were genuine Cherokees, and that this was their welcoming dance. Papa sat with his hands frozen on the steering wheel for a very long time. Then suddenly, without saying anything, he got out of the truck and took Jack and Nathan and me into Sitting Bull's. Nathan wanted a tomahawk.

The store was full of items crowded on shelves, so bright-colored it hurt my eyes to look at them all. I lagged behind the boys. There were some Indian dolls with real feathers on them, red and green, and I would like to have stroked the soft feathers but the dolls were wrapped in cellophane. Among all those bright things, I grew fearfully uncertain about what I ought to want. I went back out to the truck and found Great Mam still sitting in the cab.

"Don't you want to get out?" I asked.

The man in the parking lot was dancing again, and she was watching. "I don't know what they think they're doing. Cherokee don't wear feather bonnets like that," she said.

They looked like Indians to me. I couldn't imagine Indians without feathers. I climbed up onto the seat and closed the door and we sat for a while. I felt a great sadness and embarrassment, as though it were I who had forced her to come here, and I tried to cover it up by pretending to be foolishly cheerful.

"Where's the pole houses, where everybody lives, I wonder," I said. "Do you think maybe they're out of town a ways?"

She didn't answer. Chief Many Feathers hopped around his circle, forward on one leg and backward on the other. Then the dance was over. The woman beating the tom-tom turned it upside down and passed it around for money.

"I guess things have changed pretty much since you moved away, huh, Great Mam?" I asked.

She said, "I've never been here before."

Mother made bologna sandwiches and we ate lunch in a place called Cherokee Park. It was a shaded spot along the river, where the dry banks were worn bald of their grass. Sycamore trees grew at the water's edge, with colorful, waterlogged trash floating in circles in the eddies around their roots. The park's principal attraction was an old buffalo in a pen, identified by a sign as the Last Remaining Buffalo East of the Mississippi. I pitied the beast, thinking it must be lonely without a buffalo wife or buffalo husband, whichever it needed. One of its eyes was put out.

I tried to feed it some dead grass through the cage, while Nathan pelted it with gravel. He said he wanted to see it get mad and charge the fence down, but naturally it did not do that. It simply stood and stared and blinked with its one good eye, and flicked its tail. There were flies all over it, and shiny bald patches on its back, which Papa said were caused by the mange. Mother said we'd better get away from it or we would have the mange too. Great Mam sat at the picnic table with her shoes together, and looked at her sandwich.

We had to go back that same night. It seemed an impossible thing, to come such a distance only to turn right around, but Mother reminded us all that Papa had laid off from work without pay. Where money was concerned we did not argue. The trip home was quiet except for Nathan, who pretended at great length to scalp me with his tomahawk, until the rubber head came loose from its painted stick and fell with a clunk.

III

Before there was a world, there was only the sea, and the high, bright sky arched above it like an overturned bowl.

For as many years as anyone can imagine, the people in the stars looked down at the ocean's glittering face without giving a thought to what it was, or what might lie beneath it. They had their own concerns. But as more time passed, as is natural, they began to grow curious. Eventually it was the waterbug who volunteered to go exploring. She flew down and landed on top of the water, which was beautiful, but not firm as it had appeared. She skated in every direction but could not find a place to stop and rest, so she dived underneath.

She was gone for days and the star people thought she must have drowned, but she hadn't. When she joyfully broke the surface again she had the answer: on the bottom of the sea, there was mud. She had brought a piece of it back with her, and she held up her sodden bit of proof to the bright light.

There, before the crowd of skeptical star eyes, the ball of mud began to grow, and dry up, and grow some more, and out of it came all the voices and life that now dwell on this island that is the earth. The star people fastened it to the sky with four long grape vines so it wouldn't be lost again.

––––––––––

"In school," I told Great Mam, "they said the world's round."

"I didn't say it wasn't round," she said. "It's whatever shape they say it is. But that's how it started. Remember that."

These last words terrified me, always, with their impossible weight. I have had dreams of trying to hold a mountain of water in my arms. "What if I forget?" I asked.

"We already talked about that. I told you how to remember."

"Well, all right," I said. "But if that's how the world started, then what about Adam and Eve?"

She thought about that. "They were the waterbug's children," she said. "Adam and Eve, and the others."

"But they started all the trouble," I pointed out. "Adam and Eve started sin."

"Sometimes that happens. Children can be your heartache. But that doesn't matter, you have to go on and have them," she said. "It works out."

IV

Morning Glory looked no different after we had seen the world and returned to it. Summer settled in, with heat in the air and coal dust thick on the vines. Nearly every night I slipped out and sat with Great Mam where there was the tangible hope of a cool breeze. I felt pleased to be up while my brothers breathed and tossed without consciousness on the hot mattress. During those secret hours, Great Mam and I lived in our own place, a world apart from the arguments and the tired, yellowish light bulbs burning away inside, seeping faintly out the windows, getting used up. Mother's voice in the kitchen was as distant as heat lightning, and as unthreatening. But we could make out the words, and I realized once, with a shock, that they were discussing Great Mam's burial.

"Well, it surely can't do her any harm once she's dead and gone, John, for heaven's sakes," Mother said.

Papa spoke more softly and we could never make out his answer.

Great Mam seemed untroubled. "In the old days," she said, "whoever spoke the quietest would win the argument."

She died in October, the Harvest Month. It was my mother who organized the burial and the Bible verses and had her say even about the name that went on the gravestone, but Great Mam secretly prevailed in the question of flowers. Very few would ever have their beauty wasted upon her grave. Only one time for the burial service, and never again after that, did Mother trouble herself to bring up flowers. It was half a dozen white gladioli cut hastily from her garden with a bread knife, and she carried them from home in a jar of water, attempting to trick them into believing they were still alive.

My father's shoes were restless in the grass and hickory saplings at the edge of the cemetery. Mother knelt down in her navy dress and nylon stockings and with her white-gloved hands thumped the flower stems impatiently against the jar bottom to get them to stand up straight. Already the petals were shriveling from thirst.

As soon as we turned our backs, the small people would come dancing and pick up the flowers. They would kick over the jar and run through the forest, swinging the hollow stems above their heads, scattering them like bones.

Rick Bass
Wild to the Heart

Shortest Route to the Mountains

The trouble with buying a strawberry milkshake from the Lake Providence, Louisiana, Sonic Drive-In on the left side of Highway 65 going north through the Delta, north to Hot Springs, Arkansas, is that you have got to tag the bottom with your straw and then come up a good inch or so if you want to get anything, the reason being that the Lake Providence Sonic uses real strawberries and lots of them in their shakes. You stick your straw down to the bottom the way you do with other shakes and you won't get anything--your straw gets mired and plugged up in an inch or so of fresh-cut strawberries. So to get the actual shake itself moving up the straw and into your mouth you've got to raise the straw an inch off bottom, sometimes more, depending on who made the shake. If you've got a lot of time to kill, the best thing to do is to pull into the parking lot under the shade of the big live oak that sprawls over and cools all of the Lake Providence First Baptist Church and most of Highway 65 as well. (Years ago, the phone company had planned to nip some of the larger limbs back away from the highway because a storm might knock them down onto the phone wire, but a petition was quickly circulated and signed that requested the phone company not cut the limbs; the townspeople would, said the petition, rather do without phone service for a day or two than have the big tree's limbs pruned. There were 1,217 signatures on the petition; Lake Providence and the surrounding hamlets of Oak Grove, Louise, and Rolling Fork have a combined population of 1,198. The limbs were spared.)

Parked under the big oak, you can still keep an eye out on the Sonic because it is right across the street. The reason you want to keep an eye on the Sonic is so you will know when the lady who puts more strawberries in the shakes than the other ladies comes on duty. The tag on her red-and-white uniform says "Hi, my name is Ellen."

The best thing to do once you have ordered, paid for, and received your milkshake is to walk back over to the big oak and enjoy it over there--early August is the best month to do this. But if you are in a hurry to be off, if you are in a hurry to get to the mountains, you roll your window up after paying Ellen (you stay in your car and order through a loudspeaker--she brings it out to you and then waves good-bye and says "Come back again" when you drive off) and you move on, drinking involuntarily every now and then as a crop duster swoops head level across the highway. It is not the fastest route to the mountains, nowhere near it--the quickest and most efficient path is to jump up on the interstate and set the cruise control and rocket out of Jackson through MonroeRustonShreveportTylerDallasFortWorth WichitaFallsAbileneAmarilloRattonPassDenver. But this year I was not in a hurry to get to the mountains, because I had saved up all of my vacation and was going to squander it all on this one trip; two week's worth of freedom back in the state of my rebirth, two weeks of freedom in the state that I love most but that is, unfortunately, the least realistic state for me to make a living in. So I took the route up through the Delta. It is not the fastest route to the mountains, but it is the shortest, the best.

Even after Lake Providence is long ago a speck in the rearview mirror, the pleasant strawberry taste of the milkshake lingers, and my stomach continues to make contented little strawberry-tasting rumbles. It is sinfully pleasurable to drive through this part of the country in August with the windows up and the air conditioner on and one of Ellen's milkshakes empty in the little bag in the front seat. Because in August the north Louisiana/Mississippi/south Arkansas Delta is the most unbearable spot on the face of the earth. The humidity remains at one hundred percent twenty-four hours a day, and the temperatures never dip below 105 until after the sun goes down.

With the exception of the lean, gaunt, anchored-to-tractors farmers who grow soybeans and cotton out of the rich floodplain deposits, in August the human race disappears. Even the wildlife is missing in August; only the toughest, most ancient life forms remain. Dragonflies buzz in one place over a small irrigation ditch, sometimes just hovering, waiting for the summer to end. And like interlopers, domesticated outcasts who have no business being in this hellhole, stocky black Angus stand motionless in the few fields that do not grow soybeans; except for the ever-swishing tails, when viewed from a distance, the cattle look like thick stout china imitations placed out in the fields to break the monotony (the monotony of money-- this is the richest farmland on the planet). Only the reptiles flourish, as they always have. Red-eared sliders scramble across the sun-baked asphalt, wishing (as much as is possible for turtles to wish) that they could stop and bask an hour or two on the warm road but knowing they can't, that if they do then after about thirty minutes a big truck coming up from Jackson or New Orleans carrying a load of fryers to Little Rock (white feathers trailing behind it, swirling and fluttering in its wake) will come pounding down the highway, screaming and rattling and roaring and double-clutching and shaking the heat-buckled narrow two-lane that is already as warped as a Burma bridge, hell-bent for Eudora or McGehee or Star City or any other little town that is fortunate enough to get in its way. The turtles have learned (as much as it is possible for turtles to learn) that those of their numbers who stay and bask in the pleasant August torpor of Highway 75 are almost inevitably flattened. A few of the luckier ones are only struck on the side-rim of their flat low-slung mossy carapaces by the truck's hub, and these are the ones that, rather than being squashed, are instead sent skittering head-over-teacups off the road and back into the ditch with only superficial injuries, where, with luck, they live to snap at dragonflies another day.

There is a great deal of satisfaction to be experienced in racing past the half-turned fields of cotton and soybeans barefooted in shorts and a tee shirt at two-thirty in the afternoon on your vacation, on your way through the Delta, on your way to the mountains, being able to watch the rest of the world at work while you and only you flaunt your two week's exempt status like a hard-earned badge, like a reward. It is as if you have escaped from a prison in some clever, cunning manner; it is a good feeling.

There is also satisfaction to be had in driving past the fields and watching the tractors raising clouds of dust that, if you are lucky and are on the tail end of an early Indian summer front, drift slowly toward Jackson and New Orleans under an exhilarating mock-October royal blue sky, even in August. But more years than not, the year's first crispness doesn't come until Thanksgiving weekend, the weekend of the big games, and on August Friday afternoons like this one the dust clouds raised by the tractors blow hot and dry toward Little Rock and Memphis, or at best mushroom up around the tractor like thick fog before wisping straight up into nothing. Going north to the mountains through Lake Providence, Louisiana, is not the fastest route to the mountains, but it is the best. It gives you time to think and to prepare for their beauty. It makes them seem more beautiful when you finally do get there.

Rick Bass
Wild to the Heart

River People

Lucian Hill is a river person; he is a paddling fool. So is his wife of twenty years, Miss Ramona. Lucian's brother, Winfred E., is even worse.

This is what Winfred does every so often up in his apartment back in Kentucky: he goes to bed with all the faucets running. Kitchen sink, bathroom sink, bathtub faucet--everything. He opens them full force before turning off the lights and climbing into his sleeping bag, and besieged by the sound of crashing water, he falls immediately and blissfully into deep, relaxed slumber. He says it helps him get to sleep when he's troubled.

The only time he's troubled is when he's been away from a river too long--five, six days.

He has no furniture; there wouldn't be room for it and all the canoes and kayaks too.

He sits in his solo saddle and uses the thwarts of his sixteen-foot Blue Hole for a table, his Phoenix Slipper is his couch, and he lays his sleeping bag out in the Mad River Explorer. Winfred is thirty-seven, just three years younger than Lucian, but he's still a bachelor.

Today, Memorial Day, we're escaping the madness of Jackson as a group-- Lucian and Ramona, myself, and the ubiquitous Jim Trunzler. This is not a Sierra Club outing, not a sanctioned one anyway; it's just something we got together to do as friends. We're meeting Winfred E. in Wesser, North Carolina, at the Lost Mine campground. I ask Lucian to spell very slowly Winfred's name. Outside of a storybook, it's the first time I've ever heard of someone, a real person, being called that.

We talk and sing and eat red-hot peanuts and click the pop tops off of soda waters taken from the backseat ice chest and listen to the radio. A song by John

Prime is playing: he's singing something about old rivers that just grow stronger. We're driving Lucian's new Volvo; it's a fancy automobile, gold and shiny, with a good heavy-duty air conditioner. Our green canoes glitter atop it like noble decorations, bound for Carolina. Lucian used not to travel in such style.

Lucian is big. He's an accountant for the phone company, but he's also a weight lifter. Before Lucian married and had to go to college and learn something he could make a living with, he and Winfred used to do nothing but lift weights and work on the farm and, on the weekends, canoe. The two brothers at one time owned seven canoes, six kayaks, and a beagle. No car.

They lived in Yazoo City, Mississippi. There is no whitewater in Yazoo City, Mississippi.

What they'd do is this: they'd hitchhike to wherever it was they were going. They'd watch the news at night, and if it looked like the big whitewater rivers in Georgia and Tennessee and the Carolinas were getting rain, they'd leave Yazoo City the next day. They'd carry their boats out to the county road and sit down and wait for a ride. They were handsome devils, not too badly scarred yet, and not mean-looking at all; they nearly always got a ride. Somehow Lucian would always end up carrying both his and Winfred's canoes, one slipped over each brawny shoulder, while Win held his thumb out and carried the paddles.

Also, they were so crazy about canoeing that they'd do this: they'd get up early and paddle a long stretch of river, say fifteen or twenty miles, and then shuttle back to the starting point (again hitchhiking) and run it again, by moonlight this time. They'd just use one canoe for these night runs; they'd take turns napping in the bow while the other paddled. They never turned over, they never bumped into boulders, or took on water. They claimed it was very peaceful, sleeping down in the bottom of the canoe as it hurtled down out of the mountains like that.

One year they hitchhiked up to Vermont, to compete in the tryouts for the U.S. Olympic team; they won all their races, their times were much faster than anyone else's, but for one reason or another they never went. Lucian married Ramona, and bought a car. Win moved to Kentucky, and also bought a car. Years passed, with outstanding canoe trips the only markers instead of birthdays and anniversaries. A way of life passed with the years too--they'd never paddle again as much as they had in the old days--but they still spent a lot of time in the rapids.

It is a testimony to Lucian and Ramona's twenty-year marriage that Ramona does not know how to canoe. Today, after twenty years and perhaps three-quarters of a million miles of driving to and from the same old whitewater rivers of the southeast over and over and over, Ramona is actually going to do something other than shuttle.

Ramona is going to solo the Nantahala; she's going to run Lesser Wesser falls. She's never really paddled before--not on a river--but she's going to give it a try. She's been practicing at the breakfast-room table; she would sit in the chair and then, like flash cards, Lucian would call out a stroke.

"J!" he'd bellow.

Ramona would J.

"Cross-bow!" he'd cry. She'd swing over to the other side and pretend to dip the blade sideways.

"Rocks ahead!"

Ramona would pretend to eddy out.

"Good draw," he'd tell her, and she'd actually blush with pride, as if she'd really done it.

She's frightened of water a little, yes, and of rocks and boulders and crashing foam and surf a lot, yes, but she wants very badly to be a river person like her husband and brother-in-law.

I'm not a river person; I'm still a mountain-and-desert person, I'm afraid. I have a canoe, and I'm going to paddle, but the real reason I'm going along is to eat some more of Trunz's camp cooking. Rumor has it that he has brought eggplant along again, and I overheard him whispering something to Ramona about avocado sandwiches.

I love avocado sandwiches.

We take turns driving; we take turns buying gas. It's a good feeling, riding in someone else's car, a good-running car, with a mechanic--Jim--in your midst. The confidence and feeling of security and well-being is heightened by the fact that Jim also owns a car exactly like the one we're driving; he knows it inside and out. I sit in the back seat and nod off. Birmingham blushes in a crimson sunset.

Chattanooga. Ooltewah. Ducktown, and Isabella. Finally, Murphy, N.C. It's close to midnight; we've been driving for over nine hours. (We're river people, in search of a river.) The engine gears down; we enter the mountains of the Nantahala National Forest. Feathered black darkness and smelling-of-early-summer nighttime presses in, and wall the road on either side, and behind us and in front of us. The road climbs and winds, sinks and stretches before climbing again. We drive with the windows open. Off to our right, a few hundred feet below, the river roars.

The Nantahala

I'm up early, but so is Lucian. He's lifting a rather big rock up and down, repeatedly. I sit and watch for a while--neither of us says anything--until I tire of watching and go look for firewood. When I return he has finished his rock exercises and already has a fire going.

Breakfast is cooked; breakfast is eaten. It's a cool, almost cold, foggy morning down in the Nantahala Gorge; it's often like that, even in summer, because the gorge walls are so steep and high. Water trickles down the cliffs from a hundred different little seeps above our tents; gentle ferns and wildflowers are everywhere this time of year. Jim squats by the fire and flips another blueberry pancake; the sun rises, and filters down through twenty different stages of hardwood to land with a golden glow on our campsite. It's a fuzzy sort of morning, slow and sleepy. Everything seems to be either green or gold, soft looking, like a pastel. It's beautiful, and above all, relaxing.

Campers (fellow river people) walk down the road past our camp, headed for the river, walking downhill in lazy-legged plodstrides that belie their eagerness to get to the water. They pretend to be drinking in and basking in the beauty of the North Carolina summer morning, but I know they are faking it--I know what they're really thinking about is the rage of the river. Jim flips another blueberry pancake, and then puts another skillet on the fire and begins frying some sausage patties. Winfred E. drives up, bleary-eyed but smiling. He's short, and wiry, not at all like his brother. He shouts and whoops and gets out and dances around in the road when he sees us.

At this point in time, he'd been away from a river for almost two solid months. He had broken his arm over on the Chattooga earlier in the spring.

There are hugs, and handshakes, and backs are slapped. The pastel aura lifts; everything seems suddenly sharper. A thrush sings from the cliff; a blue jay flies through the trees. Winfred E. sits down and asks if breakfast is ready.

It's a funny river, I suppose. It's a little sad, really--it reminds me of watching a great powerful dog being chained to a pole, or something like that. It's a release-and-flow river. It's been dammed, for power, but each day it's released for twelve hours to keep the lake behind the dam from flooding, and to send power and water on down the road to others. It's a Jekyll-and-Hyde existence. For twelve hours, it's a meek and mild trickle; sportsmen fish in the little riffles, and you can see the stony bottom all the way across. It's a creek, not a river. It's like looking at it without its clothes on; it embarrasses us, as well as the river.

It makes up for it the other twelve hours. It's a wild thing, much wilder than it would be if it were free all the time instead of being cooped up half the day. It is this wildness that makes river people appreciate it so. They can, as the phrase goes, relate.

The water is usually turned on around nine o'clock in the morning. It's as cold as winter, coming out of the bottom of the deep lake, and it races down the gorge like it has something to prove, like it's afraid that each day might be its last. From put-in to take-out it is an eight-mile run, and is one of the finest in the East. It's good whitewater river; it's technical, and it's high volume, but it is also pretty clean. There aren't any sunken trees and limbs to snag and drown capsized boaters as they tumble downstream.

We wait around camp for a while, and watch the morning grow warmer--the fog lifts, leaving everything crisp looking and dripping--and then, when we feel that the first-rush crowd waiting for the release up at the put-in has gotten started, we too get in our cars and head north. We leave Win 's car at the bottom, at the take-out; we all five ride in the Volvo up to the put-in. The road follows the river. Halfway there, we notice a change in the volume of the river noise. It is much louder. We pull over and peer down into the gorge. The river has changed.

For twelve hours, it is free. We get back in Lucian's car and continue. We reach the put-in, unload the boats, and blow up the inflation bags. Ramona says nothing. I catch her adjusting her life jacket on seven different occasions. Even after she finally has it the way she wants it, she nervously continues to finger it up around the throat, like a woman feeling a pearl necklace to make sure it's still there. Her eyes are glassy, we can tell they're not seeing the soft green mountains and rocks and sky or the excitement of all the other paddlers--jeeps and trucks and cars and vans of every possible description, and people too--and Lucian pinches her behind to make her jump. She does, and yips too, and turns in outrage to see who did it. We all laugh. It wasn't that funny, but we're so excited, so tense, that we'd have laughed at anything. We carry the boats down to the water. I notice that Lucian is carrying Winfred E.'s as well as his own. I help Ramona tote hers down, then we come back for mine. Winfred E. has wandered over to a little gazebo-like stand the Forest Service has set up and is leaning against it, saying something to a rather attractive girl in blue-jean cutoffs and a halter top. She has long white hair, hair down to her shorts: not good canoeing material. We turn away for a moment, and when we look back, she is coming with us. Or rather, with Winfred E. Her name is Allison. She's from

Missouri, we find out. No, she's never canoed before. Yes, she'd like very much to try--is Winfred sure there's enough room? Winfred says he guesses there is.

We're in the water. Those first few cold splashes as you run out into the shallows, push off, and then jump in; the first couple of paddle strokes where it feels like you're not doing any good, like you're paddling in molasses, and then they begin to catch, and the canoe starts to move forward, quickly, strongly . . . the canoe itself sings down the river, like a thing released from a dam too.

We feel the same.

One of the best things about Nantahala is this: there is a good set of rapids right around the corner from the first put-in. It's called Patton's Run, and it's a good idea not to dump in it, because it'll be a long day. The sun never strikes the river straight-on for very long; it's always at least partially in the shadows, and the water's very cold. Also, it is a very long stretch of whitewater--you'll probably be washed down for as far as a quarter of a mile before it flattens out enough for you to crawl out and empty your boat.

But Ramona handles it perfectly; so do Winfred E. and Allison, and the rest of us. It's over incredibly quickly, in just a few seconds it seems, and we eddy out into a still place and gasp and pant and all try to talk at once. Our hearts race.

It's not the best stretch of rapids on the river, but it's one of my favorites. It's sure a nice way to start a Memorial Day weekend.

We're in the shadows; we're wet from the spray, and shivering. Also, we're pumped with adrenalin. We wheel out into the mainstream and push on. We race down the river like snow skiers coming down a mountain. The boats rise and chop and crash through the rocks; the boats and the river are holding a wild and joyfully angry communion together, and we're lucky enough to be caught in the middle. Lucian shouts out instructions from time to time to Ramona, but most of the time, I can tell, she does not hear them; the river is too loud, too jealous. No matter--she appears to be holding her own. Jim races past me, stroking hard. His red beard is soaked with river spray, and he is grinning madly. He does not notice me. There is an odd shine in his eyes.

I fall in a good distance behind him; I try to follow his turns, to avoid the rocks and really bad waves, but it is not until the second stretch of hard rapids that I begin to suspect he is aiming into the tallest waves on purpose rather than trying to avoid them. I draw out to one side and strike out on my own.

That's another good thing about the Nantahala: there's always plenty of people, yes, but there's also plenty of room. And traffic is fast: if you don't like it, just wait, and it will blow past you in a second. You can go where you want to, do what you want; the bank on either side, and the fact that you can't go back upstream, are your only boundaries.

Actually, when you analyze it, it's a little surprising. You really only have one choice of where to go, and that's downstream. And yet it seems like you've got more freedom that you've ever had in your life: those banks on either side, and that wall of water pushing down on you from behind are so far from your mind that they're not even comprehensible--all you can think about is the wild joy of going down, down, down the river, hard out, all the way to the end.

If you focus on the right things, and ignore the others, you can find wildness and freedom anywhere, I am convinced.

I did not notice the road that ran above us a few hundred feet, following the river; I did not notice the awesome rock quarry we passed, cut into the side of a mountain, with tiny yellow cranes scratching weakly at its base while it waited patiently for them to finish and go away with whatever it was they came for. I did not notice the rafts and inner tubes and sometimes overall carnival-like atmosphere of all the river people on the slower stretches. I focused instead on the stretch and pull of my muscles and the paddle pulling water, and the sleek way the canoe carried itself downstream, and the caddisfly larvae in the shallow pools, and the wonderfully shocking coldness and cleanness of the water, and the green and pink of the mountain laurels, and the cold clean smell that all river canyons have in their shadowy parts, and I saw not one person go by that I didn't honestly like.

In Jackson, sometimes, I'll walk an entire city block, to the bank and back, and never smile at anyone.

In some places, it is true, it is easier to focus than in others.

We had lunch in a meadow, up off the river in a wide spot where the gorge stretches to a width of perhaps five miles. There were a few other people up in the meadow picnicking also, looking down on the river, but most of them were continuing to bomb on down the river; most of them probably didn't even see the meadow.

It's good to bomb down the river, that's the best way, but for sure if you take little breaks then inevitably they'll help you rest up so when you do get back on the river you can go one hundred percent again.

Bombing is fine, but if you're going to do it, you need to do it right. You need to go one hundred percent. Even if this means doing something as sinfully pleasurable as taking a break to picnic in a North Carolina riverside meadow. There was dark beer, and potato chips, and a semidamp blanket to sit on. There were avocado sandwiches. I ate three of them, and lay back in the warm sun and I felt my stomach. I felt happy.

You would not believe what a wizard Trunz is when it comes to food. The sun was warm on my face. There wasn't any wind. I closed my eyes. Everything seemed to hang suspended, frozen: crouched and ready to go, yet also motionless, like a child playing red-light green-light. Even sounds seemed frozen; it was as if Everything was waiting for Something. The moment hung heavy as ore for a few seconds, then sighed and moved on. I sat up and watched it leave. I was ready to go one hundred percent down the river again. I looked at my fellow river people and I could tell they were too.

Also, I could tell this: that they too had felt the odd moment. It wasn't eerie, it was just puzzling, like a phenomenon, like one of those secrets of nature that you glimpse only every so often--a north-flowing river, an anomaly of gravity, an albino elk--little things She shows you only so often, just to keep you in awe, or maybe just to reward you. We chose to view it as a reward. We grinned but said nothing of it; that would have spoiled it. We pretended we hadn't seen it, so as not to startle it.

Beautiful things like that frozen-time moment embarrass easily; startle them, or study them too closely, and they might not come back. We chose just to appreciate it, not analyze it, and then we cleaned up our avocado peelings and folded the blanket and went back down the river.

Campfire. Much like the one so many years ago (was it only seven?) around which I first heard stories about Jim Bridger, about Jed Smith. I'm in the mountains again, oddly so, though who'd ever have dreamed then they'd be the tame mountains of the East? Not I, I'd have said, had someone seen into the future.

The sparks don't pop the same, the forests don't smell the same, even the pull of gravity and sigh of the wind doesn't feel and sound the same, but the camaraderie is exactly identical, almost eerily so. This puzzles me; I muse on it at length as the others toast and cheer Ramona, who successfully and even aggressively ran Lesser Wesser with grace and beauty.

Larry Cook
Opening Day

Many avid wingshooters, including me, got their first taste of hunting in the woods chasing squirrels with their dad. I hope you'll indulge me on this one-time variation from pure wingshooting.

I was only a small tyke; four, maybe five. My short legs took two steps for my Dad's one. We crossed a weed- and briar-choked field on our way to a distant ridge that promised bushytails in golden-hued hickories. Twice, Dad stopped and asked me if I needed to rest or if I needed him to carry me. Not wanting to be denied another hunting foray in the future, I bravely but purposefully replied, "I can walk daddy, I can walk." That first squirrel hunt together was a success, and my Dad loved to tell the story about that trip and the boy who would say, "I can walk Dad."

In the days before his hectic work schedule and the growth of a large family diminished our chances to hunt, Dad and I managed several squirrel hunts each season. Neither of us were fully aware of the memories these hunts generated and how in the unseen future they would comfort me and bring joyful smiles when fondly recalled.

I learned to listen for branches "shaking" as a bushytail leaped through their leafy highways; and never will I forget the sound of a "barking" squirrel. For several trips I had listened for that elusive "bark" as Dad had described their noisy chatter. Only after watching and listening to a scolding squirrel did I associate forever that shrill, rasping noise as a "bark."

Dad had a peculiar habit of easing into the woods with me in tow, finding a suitable stand, and then making himself comfortable. After only a few minutes he would admonish me to watch and he would "rest his eyes." I realize now that those were restful times for him; a chance when he could escape the stress of job, the responsibilities of parenthood, and the urgent ringing of phones--just as I do now.

While his eyes were closed, I watched for the slightest movement of a squirrel. Had it not been for my squirrel-hunting fervor, we would have gone home gameless. Upon spying our quarry, I would urgently shake my slumbering parent and point and whisper anxiously, "There, there." He would caution me to be quieter, and soon his Model 12 would roar and down would come the squirrel. He seldom missed. I remember one squirrel that was knocked from its lofty perch and began tumbling downhill. I thought he was getting away and I tore after his escaping form. I can still hear Dad crying out, "Don't let it bite you son."

Another day we were after squirrels on rocky Walden Ridge. We eased into a big hollow where there stood the remains of an ancient wildcat sawmill. At dawn a beautiful red fox raced across a rotting slab pile and, true to form, Dad's Model 12 didn't miss. For two hours I sat fidgeting and impatient to retrieve this wonderful creature. When he finally released me to gather the prize, I could hardly wait to show this trophy around the neighborhood. Deriving all I could from the feat, I cut off the fox's tail. For months it waved proudly from my bicycle.

Eventually, after getting a BB gun and extensive firearms training, I became the proud owner of a single shot Stevens 20-gauge. I anxiously awaited opening day, and after 55 years (or so it seemed), it finally came. As we eased into the woods, Dad sent me up one side of the ridge while he took the other side. Fervently wanting to get a squirrel for the first time on my own, I hurried through the woods. Why I didn't scare away every squirrel within a square mile, I don't know. Reaching a big, shagbark hickory with tons of cuttings beneath, I took a stand. My wait was short. A big gray leaped from an adjacent pine into the hickory. Even a deaf man could have heard the jump.

My pulse raced to 200 beats a minute, and I'm sure I came close to hyperventilating. After an eternity, I got a clear shot. The sound of that 20-gauge still echoes through the corridors of my mind. In slow motion, leaves, twigs, and bark showered down on me, and I heard more than saw the satisfying "whomp" of a clean-killed gray. Scarcely glancing at my prize, I seized it by the tail and ran through the woods in the direction Dad had taken. Unknown to me, however, he had taken a position only 100 yards away where he could keep me in sight. In my excitement, I almost ran past him; and until he spoke, I didn't even see him. "Got him, didn't you son?" Trying to appear cool and calm, I replied, "Sure did." Then the torrent broke and I told and retold the story. He listened patiently each time, realizing I would never again kill that first squirrel.

Dad never got to go big game hunting. He never bagged a deer or elk. If he killed a goose or duck or any other winged game, I am unaware of it. Squirrels were always his big game; and as the years advanced, a heart attack and the desire to 'piddle' in his garage and his garden took priority over squirrels. However, on rare occasions, he rode the tractor into the woods with one of my younger brothers; and what a treat it was for them to hunt with Dad.

Opening day of squirrel season is my day. I have to go . It's almost a matter of life and death. It's tradition, a link with my past. As I ease through the woods, I listen for ghostly footsteps, or peer anxiously for a dim form sleeping against a tree trunk. I hear faintly the boom of a beloved Model 12 from a grove of hickories across the field. And I wait joyously to carry the old leather game bag with squirrel tails sticking out the top.

All this is memory now. I also "rest my eyes" as I wait beneath the hickories. At the end of opening day I cut a squirrel tail, keep an empty 12 gauge shell, and go to Dad's grave. I place the tail and shell there more lovingly than any flower bouquet. If you should pass that way and see these rememberences so lovingly placed, don't think me odd. I'm remembering opening days with Dad--the way we were.

Jeff Daniel Marion
Wayside Diner

I guess sometimes I do get sort of blue, you know, the kind of feeling that just creeps up behind you like the way boys used to do me in school, reaching up and covering my eyes with their hands and saying, "Guess who?" And there I'd stand all blinded and not knowing what to say, but knowing exactly who it was by their smell. But I've got enough to do right here that I've not got a lot of time to burn--especially since Bob'd done took a spell of setting down all the time. Used to be when he'd pitch in and work right along with the rest of us doing whatever needed to be done at the moment, cleaning them tables or carrying out people's orders, or of course working on the grill--there's nobody any better than Bob on the grill. Now you take Little Bob, he ain't never gonna be the restaurant man his daddy was in his salad days, but then I guess he's got plans of his own.

Sometimes I wonder what'll come of this place here--to say nothing of the folks who eat here. Now there's them two Allison twins, been coming here long as I can remember and I been here going on forty-five year now. They won't set with one another--somebody asked Bill one day why he didn't set with his brother and all he'd say was he was particular about who he eats with. You can almost set your watch by the appearance of them two--here'll come this old black Plymouth down Main Street doing about fifteen mile a hour and straddling the center line and everybody knows just to get to one side or another, the Allisons are coming to town. They live out there on the Striggersville Road and used to work their daddy's farm til they both wore plumb out from trying to make a living. Still live in that big old two story house they was born in, but the land around there, well, it's never growed nothing but rocks anyway. Ain't been worked over in so long it'd take a passel of young men their lifetimes just to clean it up. Last thing I heard was they're thinking of selling it for some kind of mall.

Just as I get the Allisons' orders on the table--two blue plate specials--here'll come Johnny, his railroad cap tilted back on his head and grinning like a possum. I can't help but like the poor man, but sometimes he does get on my nerves, always asking about my second husband Roy--and him dead near ten year now. But it ain't Johnny's fault he's the way he is. I reckon he does the best he can, living up over the hardware store in that little old room barely big enough to turn around in. He don't complain; he's always the same, just like some six year old kid, but Johnny must be pretty near fifty or over. And I'll swear if he don't order the blessed same thing every day--"Gimme one a them big hamburgers with grilled onions on it. And plenty of mustard." Looks to me like he'd a turned into a hamburger by now. When his mama was alive and running the dime store across the street, he was always neat and clean. But now, well, law, I don't reckon he sees soap and water but once a month. Just as soon as I slide that hamburger under his nose, he'll look up and grin and say, "Bernice, how's Roy doing these days? He's a good man, Roy is. I like him. He's my buddy. I knowed his daddy way back there." And sometimes I just can't help myself, I don't want to be mean or nothing, but I'll say, "I guess Roy's doing all right, Johnny. He's out there everyday pushing up them daisies and growing sod right there where he's buried--in the Cedar Springs Cemetery."

But every time I'd say that Johnny would answer with "I never heard about Roy dying." And tears would come in his eyes before he'd look down and say, "I sure am hungry today. You fixed me a good hamburger. Thank you." So--with a scene like that how could I tell him Roy was long dead--after while I just commenced to making up answers to Johnny's question--it got to where I liked thinking up what Roy would be doing if he was still alive, and Johnny seemed to really like hearing me tell what Roy was doing. One time I got too carried away telling about Roy and said he was hauling a big load of Winesap apples out of Chilhowie, Virginia, to a market down in South Carolina. And don't you know Johnny wouldn't hush till I promised him I'd bring him some of them apples. I had to go right that afternoon over to Vine-Ripe Tom's roadside market and buy a peck of Winesaps. Lord at the trouble I sometimes get myself into. Johnny must've told me a hundred times over the next month to be sure and tell Roy how good them apples was and how proud he was to get them.

I guess Roy would've enjoyed that story--he was always giving people stuff and him and me barely had enough to scrimp by on, living in that two room apartment over the Wayside here. Many's the night I'd lay awake listening to them rats running across the attic till some big owl come in and I'd hear him get them one by one. Just a few seconds of squeaking and squealing and then it'd be quiet. Roy never was bothered by none of that--just seemed to let things go and never got his dander up. Never once did I ever hear that man so much as say a unkind word to another person.

And he had plenty of cause to--the way old man Hawkins used to talk to him when he was hauling coal for the Hawkins Hardware and General Supply. Seems like he was always pushing Roy to make better time or haul bigger loads or work some godawful shift running coal down out of Kentucky from midnight to six a.m. It was after one of them runs that I first met Roy. I was right here working the breakfast to lunch shift and in walked this country boy looking like forty miles of bad road who I could see right off hadn't had enough to eat in years and I mosey over to the counter where he's just set down on one of them stools and I say, "What'll you have stranger." He don't miss a beat, just pushes back that baseball cap and says, "Honey, I don't know what I want." I don't know what made me say it--I just looked him right in the eye and says, "Sugar, I get off work at two. Let me know when you figure out just what it is you want." And Lord, he give me that grin that ever since has just melted my bones. I thought to myself, "Dear God, what have I done here." Then he walks over to the juke box and next thing I know Patsy Cline is singing "Making Believe." I swear it was right then I knowed I'd marry that man. Course they was plenty of people had talked about me for leaving my first husband Sonny back two year before. But then they ain't walked in my shoes--or danced in them neither for that matter. What most people don't know--why it'd fill more books than what's in the town library.

So right there was the first time I ever served Roy eggs sunny side up with ham and biscuits and redeye gravy. I'd say the next twenty-five years that man downright swore by my cooking. I kept him well-fed all right--everytime he'd pass by here in that coal truck of his he'd set down on that air horn. Even now when I hear one of them trucks gearing down coming across town, I get low down lonesome and wish just once that'd be Roy coming here to swagger through that door and holler out, "Where's my sunny side sweetheart?" But I can't let them thoughts linger long, especially since it was just yesterday that Bob said he figures he's gonna close this place down, not enough business anymore and everything is moving out on the new four lane, and he thinks he's getting too old to go on. I got so blue thinking about all them years that when Johnny come in and set down right there where all them years ago Roy had set down for his first meal, I just looked at Johnny and said, "Honey, me and Roy's gonna get in that old truck of his and go on a long trip. Don't know when I'll be back. Maybe we'll just keep driving and see all the country I ain't never seen. So--Johnny, you take care of yourself and I'll be seeing you." And you know what he did? Just looked up and said, "Gimme one of them hamburgers one more time." Lord, honey, I like to have cried.

Jeff Daniel Marion
The Man Who Made Color
for the memory of my father
J. D. Marion
1915-1990

Consider the lilies, we have been told,
they toil not,
neither do they labor.

But I have sweated in the fall sun
to plant this hillside
in a cascade of hues, held
in a ring of rocks I have carried
from the river.

Long ago on my first day of school,
the teacher asked, "What does your father do?"
"He makes color," I said.
"Oh. . .I see."

But she did not see the man
who stood before vats of color
deep as flame
and dipped his finger in,
touching paper, testing the tack
of ink.

I saw him believe in the truth
of touch, the message only his fingers
would tell, color splashing
across rolling sheets of labels:
Bugler, Del Monte, Van Camp,
School Days, Lucky Strike.

Consider these lilies, Father, their color
a swash of words I roll across
my tongue--*Harbor Blue, Open Hearth,*
Spindazzle, Kindly Light. They sway
on their long stems but a day.
They know no grief, no loss,
only a tumble of color,
season to season, across this hillside.
Their blossoms unfold bright as flame,
ready for your touch.

Jeff Daniel Marion
Ebbing & Flowing Spring

Coming back you almost
expect to find the dipper
gourd hung there by the latch.
Matilda always kept it hidden
inside the white-washed shed,
now a springhouse of the cool
darkness & two rusting milk cans.
"Dip and drink," she'd say.
"It's best when the water is rising."
A coldness slowly cradled
in the mottled gourd.
Hourly some secret clock
spilled its time in water,
rising momentarily only
to ebb back into trickle.
You waited while
Matilda's stories flowed back,
seeds & seasons, names & signs,
almanac of all her days.
How her great-great grandfather
claimed this land, gift
of a Cherokee chief
who called it Spring of Many Risings.

Moons & years & generations
& now Matilda alone.
You listen.
It's a quiet beginning
but before you know it
the water's up and around you
flowing by.
You reach for the dipper
that's gone, then
remember to use your hands
as a cup for the cold
that aches & lingers.
This is what you have come for.
Drink.

Jeff Daniel Marion
Fishing at Emert's Cove in Late Fall

this morning I descended
in mist

now
my labors rest
in a willow creel
laced with fern

two small trout
to carry over the rise
to Daniel Emert's grave

we have become old friends
& once more I lay my catch
before him

overhead a kingfisher weaves
the last shallows of light
from sky & trees

held in the ring
of mountains
the only small talk
we need to exchange
is silence

the loom of days,
fabric that shawls
our winters

Jeff Daniel Marion
The Man Who Loved Hummingbirds

Once I saw my father
        lift from last fall's leaves
                below our wide picture window

a hummingbird, victim
        of reflected surfaces, the one clue
                a single feather clinging above the sill.

He cradled its body in his cupped
        hands and breathed across the fine
                iridescent chest and ruby throat.

I remembered all the times
        his hands became birdcalls, whistles,
                crow's caw from a blade of grass.

Then the bird stirred and rose
        to perch on his thumb.
                As he slowly raised his hand

the wings began to hum
        and my father's breath lifted
                and flew out across the world.

Jeff Daniel Marion
Boundaries

Get the range on these markers:

follow the branch up
to the sycamore on the sinkhole's edge
& sight left across to the buckeye stand
near the woods,
next turn right through the sage field--

you'll have to part your way
through brambles
to the white rock beside the spring.

Already you're thinking
"This is not worth it--
you're not getting anywhere."

Go ahead--pick the beggar lice from your pants.

Yoked in these lines
I mean to work this land.
What comes up won't be wasted
& what's between the rows
is welcome, too.
Maybe occasionally a green heron
will visit my pond.
I'm always at home here
still believing
the reward of this labor
is vision
honed to the blue sharpness
of ridges.

Jeff Daniel Marion
Crossing Clinch Mountain in February

I take the long road to arrival,
past barns whose weathered gray
sings the fading light.

Fields lying fallow along the way
sow dreams of a small farm
washed in creek-light,
its steady ebb
a tallow of days,

and of those cattle whose hunger
tolls them across hillside trails
to be stabled at last
beneath a dark
vaulted & hushed as cathedrals.

In this dusk
I am your single candle,
faint echo of starlight
on far mountain roads
singing the way
home.

Jeff Daniel Marion
The Egrets

October's first cold snap
     and the egrets are gone.
          All day I have thought

of them, high on the blue
     thermals, white sails luffing
          south toward a faraway savannah.

Along the old river road
     this summer the sight
          of them lifted me.

I yearned to stroke
     their downy plumes and
          long arching necks.

But they were beyond me,
     measures of grace
          held by this quiet

pool where reflection
     is water's wavering
          memory, a dream

too soon dissolved,
     rising on snowy wings.

James Still
from *River of Earth*

The following passage is taken from James Still's River of Earth, *a classic work of Appalachian literature. In this section of the novel, the young narrator describes traveling with his mountain family on a July Sunday to Red Fox Creek where they attend a preaching service delivered by the well-known Preacher Sim Mobberly from Troublesome Creek.*

An elder stood in the pulpit. He was lean as a martin pole, thinner even than Father. His cheek bones were large, angled from the nub of his chin. He lined a hymn, speaking the words before they were sung, holding the great stick of his arm in the air:

> Come, Holy Spirit, heavenly Dove,
> With all thy quickening powers,
> Kindle a flame of sacred love
> In these cold hearts of ours.

The words caught into the throats of the hearers, and were thrown out again, buried in the melody. The hollow under the ceiling shook. A wind of voices roared into the grove. The second verse was lined, the third...The elder raised on his toes, growing upward, thinner leaner.

> Dear Lord, and shall we ever live
> At this poor dying rate?
> Our love so faint, so cold to Thee,
> And Thine to us so great.

"O God, have mercy." A moan came from where the black bonnets were. I rose on the bench, looking. I could see only the beak end of white noses bobbing out of dark hoods, the fans waving before them. "O God...sinner...I am...Lord."

The singing ended. A fleece of beard rose behind the pulpit, blue-white, blown to one side as though it hung in a wind. A man stood alone, bowed, not yet ready to lift his eyes. He embraced the pulpit block. He pressed his palms gently upon the great Bible, touching the covers as though they were living flesh. His eyes shot up, green as water under a mossy bank, leaping over the faces turned to him.

"Brother Sim Mobberly," Mother whispered.

The preacher raised a finger. He plunged it into the Bible, his eyes roving the benches. When the text was spread before him on the printed page he looked to see what the Lord had chosen. He began to read. I knew then where his mouth was in the beard growth. "'The sea saw it and fled: Jordan was driven back. The mountains skipped like rams, and the little hills like lambs. Tremble, thou earth...'" He snapped the book to. He leaned over the pulpit. "I was borned in a ridge-pocket," he said. "I never seed the sun-ball withouten heisting my chin. My eyes were sot upon the hills from the beginning. Till I come on the Word in this good Book, I used to think a mountain was the standingest object in the sight o'God. Hit says here they go skipping and hopping like sheep, a-rising and a-falling. These hills are jist dirt waves, washing through eternity. My brethren, they hain't a valley so low but what hit'll rise agin. They hain't a hill standing so proud but hit'll sink to the low ground o'sorrow. Oh, my children, where air we going on this mighty river of earth, a-borning, begetting, and a-dying--the living and the dead riding the waters? Where air it sweeping us?..."

A barlow knife cut into the seat behind us, chipping, chipping. A boy whittled the soft pine. The baby slept again, and Fletch's head nodded. The preacher seemed to draw farther away, melting into his beard. Presently his words were strokes of sound falling without meaning on my ears. I leaned against Mother, closing my eyes, and suddenly Father was shaking me. He held the letter in his hands. We went out into the grove, walking toward home. A great voice walked with me, roaring in my head.

James Still
River of Earth

The sea saw it and fled...
The mountains skipped like rams, and the
little hills like lambs.

He drank the bright air into his throat
And cast a glance across the shattered thrust
Of hills: And he knew that of all men who slept,
Who waked suddenly, he least of all could name this thing
That held him here. He least could put the sound
Upon his tongue and build the spoken words
That all might know, might speak themselves, might write
In flowing script for those who come upon this place
In curious search, knowing this land for what it is.

But there are those who learn what is told here
By convolutions of earth, by time, by winds,
The water's wearings and minute shapings of man.
They have struck pages with the large print of knowledge,
The thing laid open, the hills translated.
He least can know of this.

                                     He can but stand
A stranger on familiar slopes and drink the restless air,
Knowing that beneath his feet, beneath his probing eyes
A river of earth flows down the strident centuries.
Hills are but waves cast up to fall again, to rise
Still further down the years.
                                      Men are held here
Within a mighty tide swept onward toward a final sea.

James Still
Heritage

I shall not leave these prisoning hills
Though they topple their barren heads to level earth
And the forests slide uprooted out of the sky.
Though the waters of Troublesome, of Trace Fork,
Of Sand Lick rise in a single body to glean the valleys,
To drown lush pennyroyal, to unravel rail fences;
Though the sun-ball breaks the ridges into dust
And burns its strength into the blistered rock
I cannot leave. I cannot go away.

Being of these hills, being one with the fox
Stealing into the shadows, one with the new-born foal,
The lumbering ox drawing green beech logs to mill,
One with the destined feet of man climbing and descending,
And one with death rising to bloom again, I cannot go.
Being of these hills I cannot pass beyond.

James Still
Leap Minnows, Leap

The minnows leap in drying pools.
In islands of water along the creekbed sands
They spring on drying tails, white bellies to the sun,
Gills spread, gills fevered and gasping.
The creek is sun and sand, and fish throats rasping.

One pool has a peck of minnows. One living pool
Is knuckle deep with a dying, a shrinking yard
Of glittering bellies. A thousand eyes look, look,
A thousand gills strain, strain the water-air.
There is plenty of water above the dam, locked and deep,
Plenty, plenty and held. It is not here.
It is not where the minnows spring with lidless fear.
They die as men die. Leap minnows, leap.

James Still
Death of a Fox

Last night I ran a fox over.
A sudden brilliant flash of gold,
A setting sun gilded fur
Appeared in my car's beam,
And then the fatal thump.

I asked the fox to forgive me.
He spat as he died,
I asked God to forgive me.
I don't believe He will.
Is there no pardon anywhere?

Mary Bozeman Hodges
from *Deep in the Earth*

Madeline

As John drove the Dodge delivery truck, he thought how lucky he was to be able to drive; there weren't many motorized vehicles in Outcropping in 1924. When he had first delivered groceries in the little zinc mining town, he had delivered them in a hack pulled by an old mare. Recently the company had purchased the truck, and he was feeling good to be alive as he leisurely drove down Nobb Hill.

He always drove slowly around this horseshoe-shaped row of elegant homes where the top mine officials lived. He gazed at the big windows and the screened-in porches. Flower gardens graced the large yards, and rows of flowers outlined the driveways. John loved the flowers, since at his home anything on which time and money were spent had to be edible.

As he was approaching the driveway of the chief engineer and was preparing to pull in, a shiny new Maxwell flew backwards down the driveway and into the street. To avoid being hit, John swerved sharply off the road on the right side. He hit his brakes so suddenly that he was thrown forward and smashed his face. He cursed under his breath as he tasted blood.

"These people got nobody to think of but themselves. Think they own the road. Damn lady's probably late to a tea."

He was hating the woman driving the car until a voice beside his window said, "Are you alright? Oh my, I'm so sorry."

He looked up to see a beautiful face framed in gold at his window. Moist blue eyes with heavy lashes were studying him, and he instantly forgot his anger and his pain.

"Oh, my God. I knew it. You're hurt."

Her long blond hair fell over her shoulders as her hand reached inside the truck and held his chin up so she could inspect his mouth which he was trying to hide.

"Look up at me," she said.

A fragrance which he could not recognize filled his nostrils. He thought that he must have surely died and gone to heaven.

His mouth was bleeding from the cut inside, and John was sure he looked worse than he was, but it was certainly getting him attention from this fairy-woman.

"Oh, gosh," she said, "getting in such a rush wasn't worth it."

Well, he was not so sure. Maybe it was worth it. If she would continue holding his face in her smooth hand, he was sure it was.

She opened the truck door. "Can you stand up?"

She reached for his arm to guide him out of the truck. He was amused at her concern. He'd been hurt much worse than this and had no one to assist him. But he was enjoying the attention from her, and the pressure of her hand on his arm sent shivers up his spine.

The taste of hot blood reminded him of the pain in his mouth. Turning away from her, he spate the blood out and said, "I'm all right. Really. I'm fine. You don't need to worry." He started to turn back to the truck, but she held his arm tighter.

"Nonsense. You must come up to the house to rest before you go," she demanded. "And we must clean up your mouth. I'll send for the doctor right away."

"Naw. I don't need no doctor. It's just a busted mouth. I'll wipe off the blood, and I'll be fine."

"No," she insisted. "I'll wipe off the blood and make sure you're fine."

His amusement turned to amazement. He believed that most of the people on Nobb Hill would just want to know where their groceries were and why he was on their road and in their way. He even wondered if this girl would have spoken to him if she'd not thought she had hurt him.

"Come on," she tugged at his arm.

"All right," he said, deciding he would enjoy being near her, even if it were only for the time it would take to clean up his face. "You wipe off the blood, and I'll be fine." To himself he said, I'll be terrific.

Her arm and hand were soft, and she held him with gentle firmness. She was not like the girls he knew who had to work hard. She had on a light pink sundress and pink slippers. Her flowing hair was soft and shiny, and the wind blew wisps of it onto his neck. She walked close to him and held his arm, as though she believed she were giving him some sort of support. She was fairly tall for a girl, coming up to his nose, but she was slender. Had he really needed support, he doubted her slight frame would have afforded him any security. He was afraid her hair would blow onto the blood on his mouth. He suddenly felt hot and sweaty and dirty; he decided he'd made a mistake by agreeing to enter the house. But she led him into the large airy kitchen. It was white and clean and cool, and a large fan hummed overhead. A plump black woman was busily cleaning invisible dirt.

"Oh, my Lord, Miss Madeline. Whatever has happened? This boy's hurt. Here, let me clean him up. You gonna get your pretty dress dirty."

"No, thank you, Annie. I caused this; I backed the car into his truck, and I'll clean him up. You just fix him some salt water for him to rinse his mouth out with."

Madeline filled a pan with luke-warm water and carefully washed away the blood from his chin. He could tell she was not skilled in this sort of procedure, but her touch was gentle. Not seeing a cut on his mouth or chin, she gingerly touched his lower lip and pulled it down looking for the cut. The blood poured more freely, and the throbbing in his mouth matched the pounding in his heart.

"Oh, Lord, I've made it worse!" she exclaimed.

John did not know if he felt more pleasure or pain. "Pleasure, definitely pleasure," he decided.

"It's all right," he told her. "It's just cut inside. You didn't hurt it none."

But he tasted the hot blood afresh; and, since he was in the house, he couldn't spit out the blood. He had to do something with it, so he decided to swallow it.

As though feeling his pain, Annie said, "Here, here is some salt water. Come, come over here, young man, and wash yo' mouth out in this sink. That blood'll make you sick as a dog."

He stood over the porcelain sink for several minutes, rinsing out his mouth with the warm solution and watching the blood and water swirl down the drain. He was embarrassed about having to spit into the sink. He wanted to clean the sink out, but Annie shooed him away.

When he sat down again Madeline got a clean cloth and dampened it with cool water and begin wiping his warm face and cheeks. As she gently wiped his face, he could feel her scrutinizing him. He was aware of the grey dust that was always in his thick hair, and he wished his hair were not so unruly, but at least it fell onto his forhead and covered his scar. Then he felt her push aside the hair and expose the scar; he knew she must be wondering how he had gotten it. She probably thought that he and all the mining families were rough people, and she might even be afraid of him. As a child she would've been sheltered from the people in Outcropping. She would have been sent to school in Knoxville and would've been driven there by a chauffeur along with other clean and starched children from Nobb Hill. He wanted to leave.

He needed to get back to work, and the girl's nearness and inspection were making him uncomfortable. He felt sweaty and nasty and slightly sick.

"I got to go," he blurted out. "I have to make some more deliveries before the commissary closes. Oh, and I still have yours in the truck. I almost forgot. I'll get your order. Then I got to go. I've bothered you folks enough already. My mouth's all right." He forced a bloody grin.

"Oh, but surely someone can come to finish making your deliveries for you, and you can stay and have dinner with us. By the way, you don't even know the name of the careless person who did this to you. I'm Madeline, Madeline Rogers. You might know my father, Carl Rogers. And who are you?"

Everybody knew of Carl Rogers, the company's chief engineer. In fact, everybody knew of everybody else. John knew that this girl, Madeline, had been away to school. She had just recently finished college. She was probably a couple of years older than he, and many worlds away. John had a feeling that Mr. Rogers would not appreciate a company delivery boy sitting in his home, not even now after the accident.

"I'm John, John McCullin. And, yes, I know of your father. You're very kind, but I really got to go. I might get fired." He said to himself, Especially if your father catches me here.

"Oh, how dreadful. I wouldn't want anything bad to happen to you. But I'm sure it wouldn't, would it? You're angry with me, aren't you?"

"She don't know nothing," thought John. "But I guess she can't help that. How could she know about life not being fair, living in this nice house with a maid and non-existent dirt and a nice, shiny car and the chance to go to school." If she weren't so sincere--and so lovely--he could hate her, but she was heavenly.

"No, no, I'm not mad. I could never be mad at you, and I'm real proud that you've been so nice to me. But I could get in trouble, all right." Big trouble, big, big, trouble, he added to himself.

Madeline did not give up easily. She crossed her arms and nodded her head. "Then, if you're not angry with me, I'll be at the store tomorrow to check on you."

As he floated out to the car, Annie poured a glass of iced tea and told Madeline she was going to send it with him.

"Oh, yes, Annie. That's a good idea. You're so thoughtful."

Annie went down the driveway as swiftly as she could without spilling the tea. John had started back up the walk with the groceries.

" Here, I'll take them groceries, Mr. John. You take this here glass of tea."

"Why, Annie, that's right good of you, but what about the glass?"

"Don't worry none about dat glass, Mr. John. They gots mo' glasses in that house than you and me'll ever have in our lifetimes put together. But what I really wants to say to you is about Miss Madeline. I seed the way she look at you, and I seed the way you look at her."

Annie shook her index finger at him. "Don't go shaking your head at me, Mr. John. I knows what you'se thinking, and I knows what she's thinking. She's as sweet a soul as God ever put on this earth, but she don't know nothing. Ain't never had to, 'cept what's in them books. She ain't never had to want for nothing, and she likes you. She won't see no reason why she can't see you. Oh, she knows about a person's place, but she just don't think she has to pay no heed to it. You has got to be the one with the level head, 'cause you'se the one knows about these things."

She folded her plump arms across her apron. "You knows what I means, Mr. John?"

"Sure, Annie, I understand. My head's reasonable enough. But it ain't my head that's a going crazy." He flashed her a big smile.

"You better be careful, Mr. John. Her pappy ain't so sweet as she is."

"I will, Annie, thanks. But I don't think you got nothing to worry about. She couldn't care about the likes of me."

Annie watched him as he turned to get back in the truck. He could hear her mumble, "Un, un, I sho' hopes you is right. What I thinks is that we gonna have big problems here." She turned to go back in shaking her head. "Yes, sir, we sho' gonna have big problems here."

As John pulled away, he was hopelessly in love with Madeline Rogers.

The House by the River

Often they swam; at least John swam; Madeline sunned herself. She would stretch out leisurely on the bank and always face the river so she could watch him. One day when they came to the river, it was raining. They sat for a few moments in the car, but it was hot and muggy.

"Would you like to see inside the house?" she asked.

"Go into your grandmother's house?"

"Yes," she nodded, "I'd like to show you where I spent the best days of my life as a child."

"But it's boarded up," he said.

"Can't you take care of that?" she grinned up at him. "It's not like breaking in. After all, it belongs to us, my father and me, I mean."

They walked up to the house, and, using a rock and a stick, John pried off the boards that had been nailed into the front door. They first entered into an elaborate foyer, much bigger than the one in Madeline's home in Outcropping. It had beautiful dark woodwork and an elaborate staircase. They went from one large room to another in the once elegant home with Madeline explaining every item of furniture and caressing her grandmother's favorite items. In the parlor they stood in front of an old Steinway piano, and Madeline ran her fingers over the keys, easily fingering out a familiar tune without even sitting down. The furniture was mostly Victorian, graceful and elegant.

For the first time since he'd met her, John felt that Madeline had become unaware of his presence. She was in a time and place that belonged to her and her grandmother and her mother. He was afraid to touch her; he just followed her around as she looked into old gold-framed mirrors and sat on velvet chairs and ran her hands over the material and delicate woodwork.

Every now and then she would say, "My grandfather brought this over from England" or "This is from Germany."

After inspecting the entire first floor, they climbed the rounding staircase whose dark, rich wood was now starving for oil. Madeline walked down the large hall in the upstairs to the last bedroom on the right. She stood in the doorway for an instant and then went on in. He followed her.

"This is where I used to sleep when I stayed here," she said.

The brass bed was still there dressed in a pink coverlet with ruffles on it. It looked like a child's room, like Madeline's room when she was a child. There was a brass doll bed beside the big brass bed. It, too, had a pink coverlet with ruffles on it. Madeline walked to the bed. She reached over and ran her fingers along the doll bed. Sitting down on her own bed of a time past, she looked up at him with dreamy eyes.

He moved towards her slowly as if in a daze himself. He sat beside her on the bed. She was still gazing at him. He took her upturned face in his hands and gently kissed her. Desire rose strong in him, and her passion matched his own. They became lost in their own world of dreams.

Victoria Barker
Open Ground

I know this place; the field is submerged,
Waiting. Grown high in weeds, the apple trees
Are gnarled, untended, the fruit in hard fists,
Turned inward. But it is still open ground.
I can climb the fence, move here, stalk through
The burrs, Queen Anne's lace, even carry a stick
For comfort as I wade out, maneuver in the purple-red
Of blackberry, sumac, poke; feeling my way. When I
Close my eyes, the best part comes; I smell the
Underneath side; the acrid vinegar sweet of soil and
Spring rises at my feet. It's then I can walk blind,
Stop when I hear water. Daylight surrounds me;
I can go a long way.

Victoria Barker
The Bridge

We arrived after dark to begin
The slippery climb down the hill
Toward home.
Feeling my way along a rusty wire
Nailed tree-to-tree, I let go
To grab the bridge. Its cables cold
Under my palms, barely breathing,
I slid across by inches; the swinging floor
A patchwork of shadow and light,
Ready to claim me.
Uncle once met a mad fox there;
Held his ground, kicked it off,
And shot it.
But I knew it still lived...
Up Blaine Creek, or somewhere.
I met it at every crossing,
Anticipated the rebounding step,
Tensed for the moment. "Get you next,"
He'd say. I heard the water rush beneath me;
I was already with it; washed up at the
Deep hole; reclaimed.

Lynn Powell
Rapture

I will arise and go to Jesus,
He will embrace me in his arms.
In the arms of my dear Savior,
Oh, there are ten thousand charms.

On Tuesday afternoons, the Chattanooga
Bible Study Group met in the basement
playroom and read The Revelation.
I heard the Word of God drift up the stairs.
Those nights I prayed a prayer five times
into my pillow, then saved a place for Jesus
in my bed. He slipped in late, after I was sleeping,
and still I dreamed of highwires strung up
Judgment's rocky chasms. I was saved,
but knew the *soul* baptized, not body,
made salvation take. Mother reassured me
I'd know it if it happened, but, after the revival,
I worried when alone whether cartwheels
in my chest could have been the Pentecost.

Waiting on the sidewalk for a glimpse of Mother's car,
still trembling from the goosestep of Miss Trentham's metronome,
I dreaded trumpets, quiet as dog whistles,
had called helium souls up, and abandoned me.
I could see our Oldsmobile careening,
driverless, down Dayton Boulevard, the unsaved
drivers strangely blinded to the cars of the elect
flipping upside down in ditches, and leaping,
wild and jilted, off the mountains.

Mother pulled up with a quick honk, and I rushed
to the car, but knew: some other day a blast
of change would upturn all I understood
about requirements of the flesh.

So I watched and waited and wanted to be ready
to slip through Death's hands when the dead
in Christ and saved on earth shimmied up
like July heat off blacktop.
During hide-and-seek, if the rustle of leaves grew farther,
farther, till so small it disappeared,
and the woods slipped into a strange noon silence,
I'd count *three hundred thirty three,*
then leave my hiding place and search myself.
And if our dirt-dug fallout shelter
and the shipwrecked oak were empty, and the clump
of pines drowning in a cataract of kudzu,
I'd stop and listen for Gabriel's horn--
it might be faint and maybe I'd mistaken it
for the whine of a mosquito, the faroff scream of a red-tailed hawk...
Back home, breathless, I'd start to count:
Mother, brother, then each kid who, slowly,
through the window, resurfaced in the street to pop
hot tar bubbles or ride a bike.

But on Sunday afternoons at Grandma's I'd hurry
through my cobbler, ask to be excused, then slip inside
her room to watch the picture hung above her bed.
Barefoot, He stood in the blare of sun,
angels multiplied like cumulus behind Him.
I prayed for soles like His to walk blue flames of air.
Each week His eyes followed me as I drew
close--first to memorize the river of his robe,
then closer, the landscape of hidden legs
and chest and arms outstretched, red scripture
of lips teaching me new prayers.

Stephen Marion
Elegy for Rocktown

The sheriff's car passed along the line of sycamore and musclewood above on the river road, leading an ambulance and a faded truck with a metal skiff rattling. Past the soft giggles of doves roused from their warm sleeping places in the road, past a wrecked Ford, burned out and crusted with the paper nests of wasps. Stopping at the creekmouth, the sheriff just sat there for a minute, looking out at us through his windshield, through the fog that hung over the green water and around the wet trunks of trees, and then he opened the door and stepped out and squatted down on sheets of air crackling on their two way radios. The sheriff lit a cigarette and smoked a little and flipped it away.

Who could say how far the empty boat had come? We thought of it again and again, winding slowly down beneath the railroad bridge, the rock bluffs, the back pastures where only the cattle must have stood, watching it pass without expression.

Moody Myers is gone, we said reaching down into the water for his stringer, run through the cold red gills of three yellow catfish. Moody Myers gone, and we pulled in his boat and tied it on a grapevine, and all night on the Choptack side of the river a woodpecker drummed.

It was the month of August, a sweltering rhythm of days when the world downriver lists beneath the rut of cicadas, the million choruses of frogs. Nothing can be claimed of the August gnat mists, spawned and risen in the urine smell of drying algae, the mussel shoals along the feet of islands and the sassafras thickets lashed and contorted in honeysuckle and trumpetcreeper and passionvine, the unknown limestone holes where bats exist and skim the river at dusk like boomerangs.

The sheriff knew us all. He was shaking our hands and we were telling him about Moody Myers. The old coroner and three men in white coveralls set about clanging chains and twisting ropes. One jerked at the outboard coil and it sputtered.

For every fog in August they'll be a snow this January, said Bush Lemons, who was the coroner and who boarded and disboarded gently because he had no kneecaps.

The sheriff did not pay any attention.

This here is a deep one sheriff. Wait and see.

I can't even see the other side, said one of the young men, cupping open his mouth to receive the chew of tobacco he held in his fingers. It's like the ocean.

When did you ever see the ocean? said another.

It was easy to wonder why we were all here. We thought of the town, Indian Ridge, and back on the river road the first school bus of the morning came by, perhaps the first one of the fall, a wash of yellow air in the woods. Our wives had gone by now. Our houses emptied, the courthouse and the newspaper and the real estate beginning to work without us. It was peaceful here, because nothing could be done.

Our sheriff, wearing his summer sportcoat with a gold badge slung over the breastpocket, was considering the empty boat. One corkhandled spinning rod, a handful of bent hooks gleaming like scratches in a dark puddle of leaves, an open pocketknife stuck in the wooden hull. The sheriff picked up Moody Myers' knife and examined it, as if for fingerprints. Down in their pants pockets our own hands wanted the smooth curve of a pocketknife.

Bush, the sheriff said, touching the stained blade to his mustache, you ought to take them three catfish home with you tonight.

They're hard to find this time of the year, Bush Lemons was telling us. He squinted into the fog as if it were a hot sun. They get bloated up in all of that moss. You can't hardly tell a dead man from a log or a rock or what have you. It'll be a big funeral. They wasn't nobody in Alexander County that don't know Moody Myers.

He had a leaf stem in his teeth, twisting it around as if something in his mouth were bothering him.

Hey Bush, said the sheriff. Did you hear me? Them fish are still breathing.

You know I can't eat fish sheriff. I got a descending colon. Let your wife fry them up.

The young men laughed for a second. You rarely saw the sheriff's wife. She worked nightshift, we believed.

I know he wants them, the sheriff told us. He took the pocketknife, which had one side of the handle missing, and cut a thin limb off the poketree on the bank. He shaved off a peel of skin the color of iodine and examined the pith inside. He kept a sharp knife, the sheriff said. I never saw a poke that big. What gets me about this time of the year is how the goddamn weed and all just go crazy. Big as a man's leg. It ain't civilized.

He pulled the three catfish up from the water suddenly and their tailfins slapped and he put the knife against one of their throats. It made a croaking sound, the fall belly shining, veined and scaled like the back of an old woman's leg.

He said Eat me, the sheriff told them. Eat me Bush.

Lord, said Bush Lemons, It sound to me like he's horny.

Them fish are nobody's now, said one of the young men. You ought to just turn them loose.

Probably he had heard his father talk that way.

Nobody can't eat fish, the sheriff said. I hate to see a good mess of fish go to waste.

He stood in the black silt, swinging them back and forth until we smelled the water on them, saw the whiskers and the sharp spines hidden along the dark frowns of their gills.

The outboard motor did not want to start.

Did you fill it up back yonder?

It's just cold.

Well don't flood it.

The morning had tightened around us, confined to the fathering of men and the river and the trees and the fish. Home and work did not matter. They were blind places, ignorant of the smell of soaked rocks and rotted wood and mushrooms, of the sheer chalky skin of moving water beneath the fog. We thought then of Moody Myers, drowned, his body easing in slow circles out past the county line through miles of ancient riverbed, laughing at us in our offices.

We knew this would have pleased him.

But here was the sheriff, ordering with one thin freckled arm a pattern for dragging the river, not pausing as he caught a tick laboring up his wrist. He did not consider the faint yellow collar, yoking the headsucker to the flat spotted back. Watching him flip it into the water like a seed we felt ticks on our own bodies, adrift in the tiny wilderness of skin and hair and sweat we had grown.

The pocketknife tocked back into the waterlogged boat hull.

Moody Myers, the sheriff said, looking out at the river as if he were reading the last name of a said list he had to keep. I remember when he used to take us all back in that cave down the river on the Fourth of July. There was a big rock in there that looked like Noah's Ark. He would ask us how we thought it had floated back in there and turned to stone. He could make you feel like it was a thousand years ago.

We played ball. There was some boys then that could really play ball. Nobody understood the man Moody Myers was.

I wonder where his cane is at, said one of the young men. He always carried that cane.

We'll do good to find himself, said Bush Lemons, untangling a nest of treblehooks. That's what worries me. They's places in that river where the brush is so thick it's like a tunnel. I've had snakes fall on me.

The motor fired in a boil of blue smoke, and he cupped his hands to his mouth over the noise and told the sheriff to have Jack fix them some cheese sandwiches for dinner. The sheriff started back up the bank toward his car, carrying the three catfish on already tired at this early hour, and now the sun above him was a perfect disk burning the fog, like light to a mothwing, and we could feel the day coming toward us from somewhere east of east Tennessee, the mountains already gunblued under the August haze, the ground heating up in our tobacco patches at home, those men out on the river, suffering. The sheriff motioned for us to come and we did, and behind us the boat was gone out into the fog that would become snow.

We'll find him, the sheriff told us. I can promise you that.

Judy Odom
Teachers: Please Drop
This Student From Your Roll

Give me a little time.
I can erase
his name,
the cruel shining
of his spiked
blonde hair,
my own reflection
in his mirrored glasses.
I can easily
white out
his studded leather
bracelets and his
death's head ring.
It will take longer
to remove the image
of his careful hands
against the window
as he nudged
a butterfly
toward freedom.

And centuries
of labor
will not fade
from my remembering
the gentle color
of those eyes
he did not often
choose
to let me see.

Judy Odom
For Two Black Students Sleeping
(Second Period, English 10)

I loved
your fathers
once,
those young men
walking
through the fire
and chanting
freedom.
For their sake
I cannot
leave you
sleeping
in the ashes
of that time.
You must
awaken now
into another
burning.
Raise again
the singing
of that joyous
flame.

Wendell Berry
The Wish to Be Generous

All that I serve will die, all my delights,
the flesh kindled from my flesh, garden and field,
the silent lilies standing in the woods,
the woods and the hill and the whole earth, all
will burn in man's evil, or dwindle
in its own age. Let the world bring on me
the sleep of darkness without stars, so I may know
my little light taken from me into the seed
of the beginning and the end, so I may bow
to mystery, and take my stand on the earth
like a tree in a field, passing without haste
or regret toward what will be, my life
a patient willing descent into the grass.

Gerald C. Wood
Bends in <u>The River</u>:
Hollywood's Problem with Place

In the late summer of 1983 I traveled to Hollywood to participate in a Directors Guild of America summer workshop for college teachers. One of the highlights of the two-week program was a preview of an unreleased major Hollywood feature--that year it was *Cross Creek* starring Mary Steenburgen and directed by Martin Ritt--followed by an afternoon informal interview with a few of the artists who worked on the film. Among the group who met with us teachers was Robert Radnitz, the producer of the film, who in his comments claimed a personal interest in Marjorie Kinnan Rawlings' work as *place* stories.

What troubled me throughout the forum was the difference between Mr. Radnitz's declaration and the clumsy portrait of Cross Creek in the movie. At times a powerful character study, *Cross Creek* focuses on Marjorie Kinnan Rawlings and a few other interesting people (particularly Geechee and Marsh Turner) but gives little attention to village life; mostly the place is viewed in glazed long shots. Although the film was beautifully photographed, the images fail to capture the rugged honesty and primitive self-consciousness of the place and the people I had known while a graduate student at the University of Florida in the late 1960s. Most unhappily, because the film doesn't demonstrate the relationship between the characters and their place, the voice-over in which Steenburgen explains the eternal ties between the land and its people sounds purple. The film is more convincing as a study of an emotionally sluggish woman's discovery of commitment and intimacy, but Mr. Radnitz's sense of place gets lost in the pursuit of memorable characters and the final praises of nature, which seem tacked on.

The lack of authenticity to place that I saw in *Cross Creek* continued to haunt me when I was given the opportunity to observe *The River* being shot in the Tri-Cities area of east Tennessee in the fall of 1983. The more I read about the second film and talked to people involved in making the movie or writing about it, the more I became curious about why Radnitz's ideals about the importance of place hadn't appeared on the screen in *Cross Creek*. After a while it became clear to me that the answer is found in the way films are usually made in Hollywood. Most significant in this process is the role assumed by each unit working on the project. Ultimately, this is a matter of who is given authority over certain economic and artistic choices. It is, in the strictest sense, a matter of politics.

As recent first-rate "place films" like *The Last Picture Show, Heartland,* and *Tender Mercies* have shown, a good screenplay is essential for creating a strong sense of place. Apparently there are few writers like Larry McMurtry or Horton Foote who can preserve the details, characters, and storyline appropriate to a particular place while establishing the narrative progression and bigger-than-life drama of traditional American movie-making.[1] In the case of *The River*, place was doomed from the outset, not because the story isn't interesting or true for many people, but because of the way the location was chosen. The story was originally written to take place in Illinois, but when potential shooting locations were studied, differences between sections apparently counted for very little. As the Universal Pictures publicity release notes:

> Extensive area surveys had been made of possible locations for the farm in Ohio, Pennsylvania, Kentucky, Virginia, West Virginia, North and South Carolina, and Illinois. But the location in Eastern Tennessee offered what was needed; one of the action highlights of the 14-week shooting schedule will be the staging of a flood on the Holston River that endangers the farm of Tom Garvey, and this locale was aptly suited.
>
> The flood would be made possible through the cooperation of the Tennessee Valley Authority, which at the right time would release its water through a network of four dams above the movie sight.[2]

Since the crucial dramatic action involves a river that has to be managed, TVA's willingness to help stage the scene was more important in choosing Tennessee than any qualities in the place itself. As Linda Gross wrote in a feature article on *The River* in the *Los Angeles Times*:

> Although the actual location of the farm could be anywhere, the film is being shot in upper east Tennessee, described by some of the film

makers as Ku Klux Klan and Bible Belt territory. (Visible from the highway are signs reading: "The wages of sin are death.")[3]

Unfortunately, the proposition that upper east Tennessee can be meaningfully described as "Ku Klux Klan and Bible Belt territory" will never be tested in a movie designed to be shot "anywhere."

But the cooperativeness of TVA wasn't enough to convince Universal Pictures to come to east Tennessee. Studios don't control the filmmaking process as they did in, say, the 1930's; stars, mostly because of their large salaries and popularity at the box office, are more instrumental than the bosses in getting the film packages together. And in the case of *The River*, Sissy Spacek, who is "big box office," was willing to come into the project particularly because the filming would be close to home for her (she and her husband Jack Fisk own a farm not too far away in rural Virginia). And when Sissy Spacek says she's willing to make a film, even E.F. Hutton will listen.[4]

However, all choices on a film project are not a matter of star availability or economics. Although Hollywood people see themselves as making a product to be sold, there are always artistic choices to be made along the way. Who makes these choices is the underlying political issue. On the crew of *The River* there were two superstars of the technical side who were influential in choosing Tennessee: Charles Rosen and Vilmos Zsigmond. As the production designer, Rosen is responsible for the set design and construction, as well as property management. On *The River* he decided what the farm looked like and what kind of farming community was portrayed on the location. Zsigmond is the director of photography, formerly called the cinematographer, who is responsible for the technical and artistic preparation of the camera and the correspondent use of lighting. He is most interested in the way the action looks *in the frame*. The photographic image is his responsibility and concern.

The success of their contributions to previous films gave these two men more than the usual amount of control over the artistic decisions on *The River*. Among Rosen's credits were *The Producers, Taxi Driver,* the remake of *Invasion of the Body Snatchers,* and, more recently, *My Favorite Year* and *Flashdance*. Although the quality of these films varied greatly, they demonstrated Rosen's skill in building attractive and expressive sets.[5] Even more impressive were Vilmos Zsigmond's credits not only for *McCabe and Mrs. Miller, Deliverance,* and *The Long Goodbye,* but also for *The Deer Hunter* (for which he got an Oscar nomination) and *Close Encounters of the Third Kind* (for which he won an Oscar).[6] For Rosen and

Zsigmond it was imperative that the "look" of *The River* include a natural background for the human action. They cast votes for east Tennessee because Bays Mountain would offer the backdrop that would look luxurious and pastoral in the camera.[7] Even in a profit-oriented industry like Hollywood, artistic preferences affect executive decisions--as long as the artists (in this case the art designer and director of photography) are respected by and influential with the director and producer.

It often goes with the territory of movie-making that there is a tension between the director and producer. Sometimes this conflict arises as a function of their roles. Producers have to be responsible to the studio and the "money interests" for the economical creation of their product. Directors tend to be more closely aligned with the artists themselves; they are often involved with the writers from the earliest stages of "the deal," and while they are in touch with a number of the teams who make the film, on the set they emphasize the needs and performance of the actors. The producer's responsibilities off the location are thus often at odds with the director's on the shooting lot. At other times the conflict between the producer and the director can run deeper; their visions of what the movie is trying to say or accomplish may be in conflict. Arguments left between them may force a showdown in which one or the other may need to leave the project; on the other hand, some of the best Hollywood films are nurtured by the creative compromises between these two powerful figures working on the film.

During the making of *The River* the communication between Mark Rydell, the director, and Bob Cortes, the unit producer, seemed to come easily enough, but then neither was cut out to create or protect regional or local themes and images in the picture. In the case of Mark Rydell, his background and strength as a director is his work with actors. After a short stint as a jazz pianist, Rydell attended Sanford Meisner's Neighborhood Playhouse, became a member of the Actors Studio, then acted on television in the soap *As the World Turns*, on Broadway, and in the films *Crime in the Streets* and *The Last Goodbye*. He is best known for his direction of Henry Fonda and Katherine Hepburn in *On Golden Pond* and, before that film, of Bette Midler in *The Rose*.[8] As this history suggests, he is an "actor's director," for whom the performance and dramatic potential of the scene take precedence over the image of a particular place or culture in American society. For Mark Rydell, *The River* is "a tribute to a vanishing America, the America of the Independent Farm Family."[9] He believes "'The River' is pure Americana. . .Like the 'Grapes of Wrath,' this film speaks to the impoverished agony of a whole generation."[10] His interpretation of the story thus grows out of his tendency to idealize his characters as representatives of "fundamental experience" who "can do everything. . . "

(Interestingly, Rydell sees those kinds of characters as radically *unlike* himself: "If I don't have room service I'm in trouble.")[11] The characters are not Tennesseans; they are types drawn from the American of the film tradition.

Rydell's concern with American types is held in artistic tension by the political interests of the producers: Edward Lewis and Bob Cortes. Mr. Lewis's credits include *The Fixer, Lonely are the Brave,* and recently *Missing,* all films which are concerned with the politically disadvantaged.[12] Cortes, Lewis's son-in-law, is, according to Linda Gross, a former "political activist" who remains "politically committed."[13] For Cortes, *The River* was to be less "a love story about people with strength who hold on to their dreams in spite of the odds,"[14] as Mark Rydell has termed it, than a story about senseless competition between elements of American society in crisis:

> My dream was to make a film showing how the whole infrastructure of America. . .rural and urban. . .is shutting down . . .and how independent we are.[15]

For Cortes, film is a medium for teaching valuable lessons about changes in American society which otherwise might go unnoticed by the average citizen. Big budget movies like *The River* are especially useful because they must reach a wide audience in order to make a profit. In seeking to make *The River* a parable of social and political realities, Cortes, like Rydell, would--ironically--overlook the concrete realities of the place where the film was made.

The idea of a "look" runs deep in the making of a film like *The River*. The farmhouse that Universal built in Church Hill, Tennessee, doesn't really look like any in east Tennessee, or in Illinois for that matter. As a fellow teacher observed, the roof is too steep.[16] But, as was the case with the gentle hills of Bays Mountain, the roof on the farmhouse photographs better the way it was shaped. While the gray metal tends to dominate the architecture on location, once photographed it'll look appropriate against the hills behind it. Similarly, the actors (from the Garvey children to the "atmospheres") were chosen primarily because they have a believable "look" that qualifies them to be the children of Sissy Spacek and Mel Gibson, or the caster's idea of typical east Tennessee folk. The movies are made for the untrained eye of the average moviegoer, and their visual qualities must be highlighted or foregrounded so that the eye can recognize them as attractive and true to type. The fact that movies are so visual often requires that the story be closer to the generalities of parable and myth than the complexities of any particular place. Consequently, the trees and leaves, corn and hills of east Tennessee will be seen in close-up in *The River*, and some of the faces will be familiar. But other faces will be from Hollywood; other voices will be reminiscent of Kokomo, Indiana, or of no place in particular.

The ABC television show 20/20, in airing a segment on *The River*, won the prize for carrying over-simplification about the area to the fantastic. ABC reported that making the film not only poured millions of dollars into an economically depressed region; in the process, ABC said, the film crew and the people of east Tennessee discovered a life-changing togetherness. City and country, West and South, the network reporters declared, had learned how to live together. There is no doubt, as local papers reported, that most people in the area were excited about having a movie shot in east Tennessee, getting some notoriety and money. But no area of this country can be understood in ten weeks, or ten months for that matter, especially if you came to tell the story of some other place. Some east Tennesseans resisted the outsiders and declared, "California people are not like us."[17] Others insisted that going around so much with no shoes on--as the movie-makers insisted they do--was uncomfortable; anklets would be much better.[18] And one, Anndrena Belcher, went quite beyond what the script called for in feelings of betrayal and outrage. She was hired as a stand-in for Sissy Spacek but quit after one day:

> Ms. Belcher said she was told that stand-ins would be paid more than $4 per hour that extras got, but was later told that she too would be paid that rate.

> "The whole message of the film is the antagonism between ordinary people and big business. I think they ought to practice what they preach. Some of the people with speaking parts are getting paid pretty well--about $1,200 a week, I think. But the extras are just getting used. I know it won't make any difference, but I just want them to know they can't come in here and buy people," she said.[19]

Now there's the beginning of an east Tennessee story. Hollywood movies are, after all, big business for the most part, as Preston Sturges knew when he made *Sullivan's Travels* back in the early 40's. Anndrena Belcher's sensitivity to becoming victimized, and her downright cussedness, are closer to the heart of east Tennessee than the story of *The River*.

To make a movie about east Tennessee, the story would have to come from the area, the people who make it would have to be committed to the cause of regional filmmaking, and it would have to be small, made without chasing the carrot of the common denominator of American audiences. But when the crew of *The River* came to the Kingsport area, they nicknamed Bays Mountain Mt. Rydell and later were photographed with their arms around "the locals."[20] If Hollywood wanted to make a film authentically about east Tennessee, the industry would do better by starting with Robert Radnitz's old friend Marjorie Kinnan Rawlings. The author of *Cross Creek* went to central Florida to join herself to a place, to get enmeshed in it, committed to its sorrows and joys.

> ...once tangled with it, no other place seems possible to us, just as when truly in love none other offers the comfort of the beloved....When I came to the Creek, and knew the old grove and farmhouse at once as home, there was some terror, such as one feels in the first recognition of a human love, for the joining of person to place, as person to person, is a commitment to shared sorrow, even as to shared joy.[21]

Movies with a sense of place are not made without such a commitment. Unfortunately, the hills of Appalachia have seldom been lucky enough to get such treatment from even the best talents of Hollywood.

1. Today's feature films often make convincing studies of Los Angeles or New York (and Chicago in recent comedies), but rural areas for the most part are still over-simplified in support of traditional movie stereotypes. I would argue that Appalachia is portrayed with the least authenticity of all areas of the United States.

2. "Preliminary Production Notes" to *The River*, Universal News Press Department, November 1, 1983, pp. 3-4.

3. Linda Gross, "On Golden River," *Los Angeles Times Calendar*, November 13, 1983, p.1.

4. There were also a couple of other minor factors, which in the Tennessee press were discussed as major ones. The Tennessee Film Commission courted the film industry, and Governor Alexander gave visible support to this and other film projects. Also the fact that east Tennessee is largely un-unionized and labor costs are consequently lower encouraged Universal accountants and bookkeepers, if few others, that Tennessee was a good choice.

5. "Preliminary Production Notes," p. 11.

6. Ibid.

7. Conversation with Joe Boggs, Church Hill, Tennessee, October 1983.

8. "Preliminary Production Notes," pp 8-9.

9. Ibid., p.2.

10. "On Golden River," p. 22.

11. Ibid.

12. "Preliminary Production Notes," p. 10.

13. "On Golden River," p. 24.

14. Ibid.

15. Ibid.

16. Conversation with Joe Boggs.

17. *Scott County Press*, October 12, 1983, p.1.

18. Ibid.

19. Ibid., September 14, 1983, p.1.

20. "On Golden River," p. 22, and *20/20* segment, Feb. 2, 1984

21. Marjorie Kinnan Rawlings, *Cross Creek* (New York: Charles Scribner's Sons, 1942), pp.3, 9.

Section III

A Sense of Place in the Family

James Agee
from *A Death in the Family*

In the following passage from A Death in the Family, *the young boy Rufus travels with his father and other relatives to see his great-great-grandmother. She has never seen Rufus, who is her oldest great-great-grandchild. The setting is in the mountains outside of Knoxville, Tennessee.*

"Yeah," his father said. And he bent down close against her ear. "Granmaw?" he called, and he drew a little away, where she could see him, while his wife and his children looked on, each holding one of the mother's hands. She looked straight into his eyes and her eyes and her face never changed, a look as if she were gazing at some small point at a great distance, with complete but idle intensity, as if what she was watching was no concern of hers. His father leaned forward again and gently kissed her on the mouth, and drew back again where she could see him well, and smiled a little, anxiously. Her face restored itself from his kiss like grass that has been lightly stepped on; her eyes did not alter. Her skin looked like brown-marbled stone over which water has worked for so long that it is as smooth and blind as soap. He leaned to her ear again. "I'm Jay," he said. "John Henry's boy." Her hands crawled in her skirts: every white bone and black vein showed through the brown-splotched skin; the wrinkled knuckles were like pouches; she wore a red rubber guard ahead of her wedding ring. Her mouth opened and shut and they heard her low, dry croaking, but her eyes did not change. They were bright in their thin shadow, but they were as impersonally bright as two perfectly shaped eyes of glass.

"I figure she know you," Sadie said quietly.

"She can't talk, can she?" Jay said, and now that he was not looking at her, it was as if they were talking over a stump.

"Times she can," Sadie said. "Times she can't. Ain't only so seldom call for talk, reckon she loses the hang of it. But I figger she knows ye and I am tickled she does."

His father looked all around him in the shade and he looked sad, and unsure, and then he looked at him. "Come here, Rufus," he said.

"Go to him," his mother whispered for some reason, and she pushed his hand gently as she let it go.

"Just call her Granmaw," his father said quietly. "Get right up by her ear like you do to Granmaw Lynch and say, 'Granmaw, I'm Rufus.'"

He walked over to her as quietly as if she were asleep, feeling strange to be by himself, and stood on tiptoe beside her and looked down into her sunbonnet towards her ear. Her temple was deeply sunken as if a hammer had struck it and frail as a fledgling's belly. Her skin was crosshatched with the razor-fine slashes of innumerable square wrinkles and yet every slash was like smooth stone; her ear was just a fallen intricate flap with a small gold ring on it; her smell was faint yet very powerful, and she smelled like new mushrooms and old spices and sweat, like his fingernail when it was coming off. "Granmaw, I'm Rufus," he said carefully, and yellow-white hair stirred beside her ear. He could feel coldness breathing from her cheek.

"Come out where she can see you," his father said, and he drew back and stood still further on tiptoe and leaned across her, where she could see. "I'm Rufus," he said, smiling, and suddenly her eyes darted a little and looked straight into his, but they did not in any way change their expression. They were just colors: seen close as this, there was color through a dot at the middle, dim as blue-black oil, and then a circle of blue so pale it was almost white, that looked like glass, smashed into a thousand dimly sparkling pieces, smashed and infinitely old and patient, and then a ring of dark blue, so fine and sharp no needle could have drawn it, and then a clotted yellow full of tiny squiqqles of blood, and then a wrong-side furl of red-bronze, and little black lashes. Vague light sparkled in the crackled blue of the eye like some kind of remote ancestor's anger, and the sadness of time dwelt in the blue-breathing, oily center, lost and alone and far away, deeper than the deepest well. His father was saying something, but he did not hear and now he spoke again, careful to be patient, and Rufus heard, "Tell her 'I'm Jay's boy.' Say, 'I'm Jay's boy Rufus.'"

And again he leaned into the cold fragrant cavern next to her ear and said, "I'm Jay's boy Rufus," and he could feel her face turn towards him.

"Now kiss her," his father said, and he drew out of the shadow of her bonnet and leaned far over and again entered the shadow and kissed her paper mouth, and the mouth opened, and the cold sweet breath of rotting and of spice broke from her with the dry croaking, and he felt the hands take him by the shoulders like knives and forks of ice through his clothes. She drew him closer and looked at him almost glaring, she was so filled with grave intensity. She seemed to be sucking on her lower lip and her eyes filled with light, and then, as abruptly as if the two different faces had been joined without transition in a strip of moving-picture film, she was not serious any more but smiling so hard that her chin and her nose almost touched and her deep little eyes giggled for joy. And again the croaking gurgle came, making shapes which were surely words but incomprehensible words, and she held him even more tightly by the shoulders, and looked at him even more keenly and incredulously with her giggling, all but hidden eyes, and smiled and smiled, and cocked her head to one side, and with sudden love he kissed her again. And he could hear his mother's voice say "Jay," almost whispering, and his father say, "Let her be," in a quick, soft, angry voice, and when at length they gently disengaged her hands, and he was at a little distance, he could see that there was water crawling along the dust from under her chair, and his father and his Aunt Sadie looked sad and dignified, and his mother was trying not to show that she was crying, and the old lady sat there aware only that something had been taken from her, but growing quickly calm, and nobody said anything about it.

Jeff Daniel Marion
Orpha

she came daily
past us
to rusting mailboxes
lined like loaves

the bitter bread
no word, no letter
from distant kin

inside, warmed
we watched
while the sky spit
snow

that winter
she died
they brought her son home
from the state
penitentiary

what memory restores
to us
a grave, mound of earth
loaf,
our daily bread

Jeff Daniel Marion
My Grandmother Sifting

years of the world's distance
glazed
behind panes of darkness

now
near the cupboard
she goes by the feel
of flour sifting

touch by touch
the world enters here
descending in whiteness
across her hands

a winter sky shakes itself loose:
drift of last summer's
dust in a cold season

where morning stokes its light
across her sills
in patchwork

alone daily
she
breaks this bread

Jeff Daniel Marion
J.D.M.

Remembering their names
my father recounts the days,
each one mapped deep
in his memory. He believes
I remember them all,
have known them in my own way.

Listening, I settle back
and find the places in his voice:
an old cemetery, its gate rusty,
air heavy with the incense of cedars.
He names those friends once more
and I choose the grave stone
for each, study the lines growing faint.

Savoring the tales he tells,
he resurrects them one by one.
They do a strange dance
shaped by his words
and for a moment I believe
I knew them, shared their days.

We turn off the main road,
wind back in the mountains
toward Galbraith Springs.

People came from far places
believing this water a cure.
As a boy he and his friends came here
to sell blackberries and listen
to stories of other places,
a map of the world growing wider
summer by summer.

No one comes here much anymore.

But this is his place:
quiet and forgotten,
his youth lies buried here,
marked only by his initials
carved into a wooden bench
set beside the spring.

We eye one another across shadows
darkening the spring. We search for
some word that could cure,
heal us now in this moment passing.
The only sound is the spring, quietly flowing.

He kneels, cups his hands to drink
and believes what he has always told me:
"Some springs never go dry."

Rita Quillen
October Dusk
(for Mac)

The evening dark
falls all around me,
its warm breath
casts a shadow on my face.

Sitting on my front steps,
I am a candle flame
drawing moths and mosquitoes,
holding the moments in my cupped hands.
He sits quietly by me,
memories of the day's work
swift moving color shared
like fall leaves in the yard.

The potatoes from the garden
lie scattered in the grass.
Tomorrow we will sort them
and store them for winter.

His hand rests on my neck
as he slowly stands.
He offers the other dirty hand
to help me up.

Our eyes meet in the fading light.
We go inside,
surrendering to night,
the smell of earth still strong.

Rita Quillen
My Daughter's Popsicles

I break the popsicle in half
She begins in the middle
where it is already cracked
red syrup
spreading to her elbows.
She swaps licks with her cat,
watching her treat grow smaller.
The last bite
is smeared onto the porch,
used to starch her curls,
take the cat's pawprints.
The stick becomes a baton
for my little conductor
who will learn
within a year or two
to eat popsicles from the end,
keep the sugary syrup
all in her mouth
and conduct
herself.

Rita Quillen
Revival

A musky sweat smell
filled the room
faces looked for Jesus' picture.
I stood by mother
in an organdy dress bought for Easter.

The preacher spit words
I didn't understand
about a fiery pit
Satan's work.
Many moaned, cried
said Yes Lord.
I squeezed my dress into little pleats,
my moist hands staining dark prints.

Suddenly
a neighbor man who walked with lowered eyes
and rarely spoke
yelled and jumped out into the aisle,
his red-rimmed wild eyes glassy.
The preacher's eyes bulged from his stubbed face.
Heed the Holy Spirit.

The neighbor man raised his arms high
and hopped on one foot,
then the other.
I sat on the front row
under the shadow of his ranting
while a low jabbering from the back
spread forward louder and louder
until a woman screamed.
I turned from mother
who was whispering with closed eyes and
ran out of the shadow into the clean night air.

Kathryn Stripling Byer
from *Wildwood Flower*

Lineage

This red hair
I braid while she
sits by the cookstove
amazes her. Where
did she get hair the color
of wildfire, she wants to know,
pulling at strands of it
tangled in boar-bristles.
I say from Sister, God knows
where she is, and before
her my grandmother you
can't remember because
she was dead by the time
you were born, though you hear
her whenever I sing,
every song handed down
from those sleepless nights
she liked to sing through
till she had no time
left for lying awake
in the darkness and talking
to none save herself.

And yet, that night
I sat at her deathbed
expecting pure silence,
she talked to dawn
when at last her voice
failed her. She thumbed out
the candle between us
and lifted her hand
to her hair as if what
blazed a lifetime might still
burn her fingers. Yes,
I keep a cinder of it
in my locket I'll show you
as soon as I'm done telling
how she brought up from
the deep of her bedclothes
that hairbrush you're holding
and whispered, "You
might as well take it."

Kathryn Stripling Byer
from *Wildwood Flower*

Cobwebs

From the table where
I sit dressed up
for church, my bonnet
pulled down to my
eyebrows and my dinner
basket proper on my knees,
I frown against the sun
that, free of clouds
a moment, makes the cobwebs
strung between my
porch rails shimmer.
Signs! God's signs
hide everywhere like
hooks. Like trap
lines in the current
snaring some bright
pattern I can't see
for looking out the wrong
way or not looking
while I sit here,

scrubbed and corseted
for Easter's singing
of the old Arise
and See His Glory
climbing up the hills
of morning like these
cobwebs sun might turn
to Jacob's Ladders
if I let it through
my squinted eyes.

Kathryn Stripling Byer
from *Wildwood Flower*

Easter

Where my father's house stood
at the edge of the cove is a brown church
the faithful call Bosom of God.
I have come back to sit at the window
where I can see apple trees bud
while the preacher shouts death has no victory.

Everywhere dogwoods are blooming
like white flesh this man claims
is devil's work: woman who tasted
the apple and disobeyed God. But for Christ
we are doomed to the worms waking under
these hills I would rather be climbing

again with my father's goats bleating
so loud I can't hear this man say
I must ask the Lord pardon for what
I've come to remember--the sun
on my neck as I shook loose my braids
and bent over the washpot. My bare feet

were frisky. If wind made the overalls
dance on the clothesline, then why
shouldn't I? Who's to tell
me I should not have shouted for joy
on this hill? It's the wind I praise God for
today, how it lifted my hair like a veil.

Judy Odom
Kevin

For you
I should've tried
a rap song.
That would surely please you.
But I wasn't raised for rapping
like Run DMC.
I can't quite catch the beat.
I don't like rhyming.
And besides,
I've lived too long
here in these mountains
to feel easy
making poems out of broken
glass
and ghetto jive
and wild erratic horns.
But you,
my son,
you walk the ridges
dreaming asphalt.

The clean smell of pine trees
sets you longing
for hot gasoline
and melting tar
and diesel fumes.
You contemplate the mist
that settles in the hollows
and imagine buildings
moored in L.A. smog.
And so,
I give you what I can--
this poem
blending dulcimers
and drums
and keyboard synthesizers.
I sing you
red-winged maple seeds
and dark smoke
drifting
on the same free wind.

Judy Odom
*For One Who Should
Have Been My Daughter*

You are not mine
in blood or bearing.
I may claim you
only as I call
my own
an afternoon
of summer light
remembered
or the music
of an unseen flute
played sweet
and high
and lonesome
drifting gently
through my open window
in the dark.

Like intricate
leaf shadows
on a moonlit wall

or the exuberant
true color
of forsythia
in spring,
you offer me
a grace
I had
no part
in making,
a balance
and completeness
I may
recognize
but have
no word
or right
to name.

Denise Giardina
from *Storming Heaven*

In the following passages from the novel Storming Heaven, *by the West Virginia writer Denise Giardina, the character Rondal Lloyd remembers two important events from his childhood. He grew up in the coal camps of West Virginia where poverty was standard and where even young children were forced to go to work in the mines under horrible conditions. For Rondal Lloyd, childhood was brief. The time is the early part of this century.*

I attended the Winco School and did well. When I was in the third grade, the teacher, Miss Radcliffe, invited the ten best students to her apartment for oatmeal cookies. She lived in the clubhouse, a building most of us had never entered. It was reserved for the unmarried teachers, nurses, and bookkeepers of the company.

Miss Radcliffe, tall and gray-headed, led us single-file up the stairs and ushered us into her rooms with the air of a genie revealing a treasure. We tiptoed across a rug Miss Radcliffe said was oriental and settled in miserable silence upon her purple-striped sofa and chairs. Miss Radcliffe smiled proudly as we craned our heads to take in the high cherry bookcases with glass doors, the purple flowered wallpaper, the grandfather clock with gold trim on the door.

She served the cookies on bone-white china, and we had hot tea served in delicate cups with handles so small that even a child could not get a proper grip without being burned. Miss Radcliffe talked about the importance of an education, about how we had the obligation to raise ourselves above our parents and save our mountain people from ignorance. She reminded us that Abraham Lincoln had been as poor as we were. Then she gave us our assignments for Class Day, when our parents would visit the school. I was to memorize the first two paragraphs of The Declaration of Independence.

Cookie crumbs kept falling down the front of my overalls and I couldn't fish them out without spilling my tea. I was afraid they would drop on Miss Radcliffe's carpet when I stood up, and she would call me "slovenly," one of her favorite terms of disdain. When the grandfather clock struck four, we escaped. I wrapped three cookies in my bandanna to share with my brothers after supper, and ran down the hill to our house. When I went inside, I smelled grease. Mommy was scraping the bacon leavings in the iron skillet for gravy. I scuffed my bare feet across the gritty wood floor, sprinkled with coal dust despite Mommy's daily scrubbings. Yellowing newspapers plastered the wall to keep out the cold.

Talcott and Kerwin wrestled on the bed in the front room.

"Yall lookee here," I said. "I got a surprise treat for after supper."

When they reached for the bundle I held it high above my head.

"After supper," I said.

I stuck the cookies beneath my pillow, dared them to touch it. Then to show I was not so strict, I hugged Talcott to me and tickled his belly. He wriggled and laughed. The back of his neck smelled of dried perspiration, sweet like a field in summertime. I sighed, lay back on the bed, and was glad to be home.

Denise Giardina
from *Storming Heaven*

(Note comments on previous reading)

I knew there were other children in the mine. Boys at my school were always dropping out to go to work. I would lose sight of them for weeks, then they would reappear on a Sunday afternoon, some with chaws of tobacco bulging in their cheeks, looking hard and wise like little old men. I felt ashamed when I thought of them. Daddy was right. I was due no special privileges.

I knew the boy on the first trap door we came to. He was an Italian who went to first grade with me. His job was to pump the trap door all day long, keep the air moving. He had to open the door for the mule trains, too, and keep out of the way so he wouldn't be run down. When the light from my cap reached his door, I saw he had been writing on it with slate. DO NOT SCARE THE BIRDS, he had scrawled, and beneath that a picture of a canary with fancy swirls on its wings. I raised my hand to him. He nodded briefly as he hauled on the door.

We walked almost two miles in. It was low coal so that Daddy and his buddy must always crawl, but I was short for my age and could walk if I bent over. I was called on to fetch and carry the tools, the auger, rod and black powder. Daddy stretched out on his belly and showed me how they would work.

"This is called our place and that there is the face of the coal. We drill in there with our auger and then we tamp in the powder and dirt and the needle. Tamp it in tight as a virgin's ass. Then we pull out the needle and stick the squib in the hole and light it. Then we git for cover on our hands and knees. You stay put out of the way while that's going on. You'll help us load the coal after it blows."

Daddy's buddy, Joe Kracj, crawled in and was listening but not understanding a word. He was a foreigner. I couldn't see his face in the dark because of the carbide lamp on his head, and it occurred to me that I work with him all day and never recognize him outside the mine.

"You git down when the coal starts to blow," Daddy said. "Put your head down. You'll know hits a-coming when I holler out like this."

He leaned back and yelled, "Fi-i-i-yah! Fire in the hole!"

He laughed. "I allays do the hollering cause hit just don't sound right when ole Joe does it."

I went back where Daddy showed me to wait while they drilled. I tried not to think of the mountain pushing down on us. To distract myself, I bobbed my head up and down and watched the light from my lamp skitter across the ribs and timbers. It was quieter than I had expected. Puffs of coal dust danced in my lamplight. I heard a steady plopping of water, like a darkness. I longed to see the mine lit just once, to possess a magical eyesight that could see the men all at their places; Daddy crawling on his belly in the number four coal; others drilling upright in the number five; the skinners driving their mules; the trappers opening and closing the trap doors. I felt them trying to breathe together as one, in unison with my own heaving chest. The air was still and our breathing could not move it. The mountain pressed down, uneasy at the violation of its entrails. Daddy hollered. The air blew apart. I bounced onto my belly, covered my ears with the heels of my hands. The earth stroked my chest, my thighs.

Daddy emerged from a billowing black cloud.

"Come on, boy, time to break it up and load it."

I jumped up and hit my head on the roof.

When we left the mine at the end of the day I was so weary from shovelling coal that I could not walk very fast. When we came for Talcott, he could not stand up, but sat hunched over on his bench. Daddy picked him up and he cried out.

"Don't worry, son," Daddy said. "You'll git toughened up."

I heard Mommy crying in the kitchen that night before I slept.

"What am I supposed to do? I'm a-scairt to hug my own babies for fear of hurting them. I seen bruises all over Talcott's back where that boss man hit on him. Ain't no mother supposed to let such things happen to her younguns."

"Shut up!" Daddy said. "I can take care of them boys."

I closed my eyes.

The pain in my body settled into a dull ache. I went on. For the first time in memory, I spent time with my daddy. I came to realize that he was glad to have me with him. He had few ways of showing it. We seldom spoke underground. We were too busy with our picks and shovels, straining to load as many tons as we could, for the more we loaded, the more we were supposed to earn. But when we left the mine, Daddy sometimes pulled off my cap and gently rubbed his knuckles back and forth across the top of my head. He could never bring himself to touch me with the fleshy palms of his hands. But I knew he loved me.

It was Mommy I missed now. I only saw her on Sundays, except for a few moments in the early morning and late at night. Even on Sundays she seemed more distant. She went to church and stayed all morning, or worked in the garden and told me not to come bother her.

On Sunday when she was outside, I got the idea of reading the newspapers covering the walls. I missed C.J.'s visits with the Justice Clarion, missed the books at school. The newspapers were new; Mommy had put them up that very week. I brought a wooden chair from the kitchen and set it by the front door, lit a kerosene lantern, and stretched on tiptoe to read the headlines near the ceiling. When I had read halfway down the wall, I got down and stood on the floor, then worked my way around the room, even removed the calendar with the picture of Jesus given out by Ermel Justice's store so I could read beneath it. I was wedged in tight behind the black pot-bellied stove, my rear end pressed against the pipe, engrossed in an account of how European companies would soon be mining coal in China, when there came a sizzle and pop and a burst of acrid smoke. The heat from the lantern's chimney had set the wall on fire.

I squirmed from behind the stove, ran outside to the rain barrel, returned with a bucket of water. I dashed the water against the wall. A gaping black-edged hole was left in Mommy's clean newsprint wallpaper, but the flames were dead.

I went to find her in the garden.

"What you doing down here?" she said. She was clearing a patch for fall planting.

I told her what I had done. When she didn't answer, I said, "You going to switch me?"

"Why should I?" She chipped at the ground with her hoe. "You done gone in the mines. Ain't no switch going to faze you none. Your daddy done made a man outen you. I cant do nothing with you now."

I wished she would whip me about the bare legs with a briar switch, like in the old days, then weep at the sight of the scratches, hug me and feed me an apple butter biscuit. But I was left lonesome to chastise myself.

Pat E. Salyer
Paper Love

At some time in forty years
my mother must have hugged me.
If so, it left no impression.
She gathers cucumbers
and ripe tomatoes from her garden,
sending them to me
in dew-damp paper sacks.
A new subscription starts;
my husband carries *Southern Living*
from the mailbox and announces,
"It's your mother again."
She clips articles
from *The Upper Room* and *Grit*
then mails them to me
inside Helen Steiner Rice cards.

After our monthly trips to her doctor,
I sometimes find
a crumpled twenty stuffed
in the side of my purse.
I wished for an arm on my shoulder,
something more than I had,
until I came to understand
that brown-bagged cucumbers
are a communication.
Now I swallow them greedily,
can't ever get enough, and
I've been thinking that I must
write a note
to let my mother know
that I've finally got her message.

Pat Salyer
Clinging to the Roots

I swore I'd never marry a farmer.
Got tired of hearing every Saturday,
"You big girls get out of bed and
help your Momma. The beans have to
be picked and the tomatoes canned."
Hated worrying about every hailstorm
and dry spell threatening the tobacco
crop and the possibility of a new dress.
Couldn't abide eating the same pig
I'd slopped for months, hog-killing day,
and everything greasy for a week.
I'd marry a city boy, buy my green beans
in a can at the air-conditioned
Kroger store and bring home faceless
pork on a styrofoam tray. Sleep
half-a-day on Saturdays and have
a regular paycheck...a better life.

I thought I'd left it all behind, but
as I turn forty, I find that
I want the earth still clinging
to the little new potatoes Momma
gives me, and early Saturday mornings
I shop the Farmer's Market
for fresh green beans.
The paychecks aren't
regular enough when the plant
lays off, and I silently belittle
the worth of my city man
who doesn't know how to stake
the yellow tomatoes I grow
in the flower bed.

Pat Salyer
Muddy Creek Ritual

On Muddy Creek...
        the snap of a screen door
        draws five waiting children
        from the blurry-eyed Zenith.
        A khaki man stands
        in a patch of linoleum flowers
        and holds out a paper sack
        to the cottonheads gathering
        around his legs.
        He smiles over their heads
        at a woman quietly watching
        as she breaks beans
        for tomorrow's dinner.

        Every Saturday night
        he spends a couple of hours
        shooting the bull at Cooper's Esso,
        bagging six candy bars
        to bring home.

Eager hands slide
into Saturday's grab-bag
fingering chocolate squares,
almond ovals and peanut ridges--
each seeking his own sweet share.

Wrapper rattle signals
ritual's consumption.
He moves closer to his woman
sliding a thin Heath bar
and pleasure-bent fingers
into her warm pocket.
"I'll take *my* sweetenin' later,"
he whispers.

She lifts Saturday's child
to her hip and smiles wearily,
wondering at the price of sugar.

Fred Chappell
from *I Am One of You Forever*

The Overspill

Then there was one brief time when we didn't live in the big brick house with my grandmother but in a neat two-story green-shingled white house in the holler below. It was two storeys if you stood at the front door; on the other side it was three storeys, the ground floor a tall basement garage.

The house was surrounded by hills to the north and east and south. Directly above us lay the family farm and my grandmother's house. Two miles behind the south hill was the town of Tipton, where the Challenger Paper and Fiber Corporation smoked eternally, smudging the Carolina mountain landscape for miles. A small creek ran through our side yard, out of the eastern hills. The volume of the creek flow was controlled by Challenger; they had placed a reservoir up there, and the creek water was regulated by means of the spillway.

At this time my mother was visiting her brother in California. Uncle Luden was in trouble again, with a whole different woman this time. Maybe my mother could help; it was only 5,000 miles round trip by train.

So my father and I had to fumble along as best we could. Despite the extra chores, I found it exciting. Our friendship took a new and stronger turn, became something of a mild conspiracy. New sets of signals evolved between us. We met now on freshly neutral ground somewhere between my boyhood and his boyishness, and for me it was a heady rise in status. We were clumsy housekeepers, there were lots of minor mishaps, and the tagline we formulated soonest was: "Let's just not tell Mama about this one." I adored that thought.

He was always dreaming up new projects to please her and during her absence came up with one of masterful ambition.

Across the little creek, with its rows of tall willows, was a half-acre of fallow ground considered unusable because of marshiness and the impenetrable clot of blackberry vines in the south corner. My father now planned it as a garden, already planted before she returned.

We struggled heroically. I remember pleasantly the destruction of the vines and the cutting of the drainage ditch neat and straight into the field. The ground was so soft that we could slice down with our spades and bring up squares of dark blue mud and lay them along side by side. They gleamed like tile. Three long afternoons completed the ditch, and then my father brought out the big awkward shoulder scythe and whetted the blade until I could hear it sing on his thumb ball when he tested it. And then he waded into the thicket of thorny vine and began slashing. For a long time nothing happened, but finally the vines began to fall back, rolling in tangles like barbarous handwriting. With a pitchfork I worried these tangles into a heap. Best of all was the firing, the clear yellow flame and the sizzle and snap of the vine-ribs and thorns, and the thin black smoke rising above the new green willows. The delicious smell of it.

After this we prepared the ground in the usual way and planted. Then we stood at the edge of our garden, admiring with a full tired pride the clean furrows and mounded rows of earth.

But this was only a part of the project. It was merely a vegetable garden, however arduously achieved, and we planted a garden every year. My father wanted something else, decorative, elegant in design, something guaranteed to please a lady.

The weather held good and we started next day, hauling two loads of scrap lumber from one of the barns. He measured and we sawed and planned. He hummed and whistled as he worked and I mostly stared at him when not scurrying to and fro, fetching and carrying. He wouldn't, of course, tell me what we were building.

On the second day it became clear. We were constructing a bridge. We were building a small but elaborate bridge across the little creek that divided the yard and the garden, a stream that even I could step over without lengthening my stride. It was ambitious: an arched bridge with handrails and a latticework arch on the garden side enclosing a little picket gate.

He must have been a handy carpenter. To me the completed bridge appeared marvelous. We had dug deep on both sides to sink the locust piers, and the arch above the stream, though not high, was unmistakably a rainbow. When I walked back and forth across the bridge I heard and felt a satisfactory drumming. The gate latch made a solid cluck and the gate arch, pinned together of old plaster lathe, made me feel that in crossing the bridge I was entering a different world, not simply going into the garden.

He had further plans for the latticework. "Right here," he said, "and over here, I'll plant tea roses to climb up the lattice. Then you'll see."

We whitewashed it three times. The raw lumber sparkled. We walked upstream to the road above the yard and looked at it, then walked downstream to the edge of the garden and looked at it. We saw nothing we weren't prideful about.

He went off in our old Pontiac and returned in a half hour. He parked in the driveway and got out. "Come here," he said. We sat in the grass on the shoulder of the culvert at the edge of the road. "I've been to the store," he said. He pulled a brown paper sack from his pocket. Inside I found ten thimble-shaped chocolate mints, my favorite. From another pocket he produced a rolled band of bright red silk.

"Thank you," I said. "What's that?"

"We want her to know it's a present, don't we? So we've got to tie a ribbon on it. We'll put it right there in the middle of the handrail." He spooled off two yards of ribbon and cut it with his pocket knife. "Have to make a big one so she can see it from up here in the road."

I chewed a mint and observed his thick horny fingers with the red silk.

It was not to be. Though I was convinced that my father could design and build whatever he wished--the Brooklyn Bridge, the Taj Mahal--he could not tie a bow in this broad ribbon. The silk crinkled and knotted and slipped loose; it simply would not behave. He growled in low tones like a bear trying to dislodge a groundhog from its hole. "I don't know what's the matter with this stuff," he said.

Over the low mumble of his words I heard a different rumble, a gurgle as of pebbles pouring into a broad still pool. "What's that?" I asked.

"What's what?"

"What's that noise?"

He stopped ruining the ribbon and sat still as the sound grew louder. Then his face darkened and veins stood out in his neck and forehead. His voice was quiet and level now. "Those bastards."

"Who?"

"Those Challenger Paper guys. They've opened the floodgates."

We scrambled up the shoulder into the road.

As the sound got louder it decomposed into many sounds: lappings, bubblings, ripplings, undersucks, and splashovers. Almost as soon as we saw the gray-brown thrust of water emerge from beneath the overhanging plum tree, we felt the tremor as it slammed against the culvert, leaping up the shoulder and out of a hose. In a few seconds it had overflowed the low creek banks and streamed gray-green along the edge of the yard, furling white around the willow trunks. Debris--black sticks and leaves and grasses--spun on top of the water, and the gullet of the culvert rattled with rolling pebbles.

Our sparkling white bridge was soiled with mud and slimy grasses. The water driving into it reached a gray arm high into the air and slapped down. My father and I watched the hateful battering of our work, our hands in our pockets. He still held the red ribbon and it trickled out of his pocket down his trouser leg. The little bridge trembled and began to shake. There was one moment when it sat quite still, as if it had gathered resolve and was fighting back.

And then on the yard side it wrenched away from the log piers, and when that side headed downstream the other side tore away too, and we had a brief glimpse of the bridge parallel in the stream like a strange boat and saw the farthest advance of the flood framed in the quaint lattice arch. The bridge twirled about and the corners caught against both banks and it went over on its side, throwing up the naked underside of the planks like a barn door blown shut. Water piled up behind this damming and finally poured over and around, eating at the borders of the garden and lawn.

My father kept saying over and over, "Bastards, bastards, bastards. It's against the law for them to do that."

Then he fell silent.

I don't know how long we stared downstream before we were aware that my mother had arrived. When we first saw her she had already got out of the taxi, which sat idling in the road. She looked odd to me, wearing a dress I had never seen, and a strange expression--half amused, half vexed--crossed her face. She looked at us as if she'd caught us doing something naughty.

My father turned to her and tried to speak. "Bastards" was the only word he got out. He choked and his face and neck went dark again. He gestured toward the swamped bridge and the red ribbon fluttered in his fingers.

She looked where he pointed, and as I watched, understanding came into her face, little by little. When she turned again to face us she looked as if she were in pain. A single tear glistened on her cheek, silver in the cheerful light of midafternoon.

My father dropped his hand and the ribbon fluttered and trailed in the mud.

The tear on my mother's cheek got larger and larger. It detached from her face and became a shiny globe, widening outward like an inflating balloon. At first the tear floated in air between them, but as it expanded it took my mother and father into itself. I saw them suspended, separate but beginning to drift slowly toward one another. Then my mother looked past my father's shoulder, looked through the bright skin of the tear, at me. The tear enlarged until at last it took me in too. It was warm and salty. As soon as I got used to the strange light inside the tear, I began to swim clumsily toward my parents.

Karen Walden Simpson
Knitting Memories

"Hey, are you asleep?...*I said are you asleep?*"

Nannie (so named because when my mother was a toddler, "Granny" came out "Nannie") has never understood how any self-respecting soul could sleep past 8 A.M.--and few ever have in her presence--but I always enjoyed our visits enough not to resent it too much.

"Come sit down," she'd say, patting the sunlit piece of couch beside her. And there we would sit and talk while she worked on her knitting and helped me learn on some extra needles. "Through...over...under...off," we'd practice, just as her grandfather (Grandsir, as she called him) had taught her. Sometimes, when I'd become bored with knitting (as might be expected of a six-year-old on summer vacation), we would wind some of her new skeins of thread into balls. I never liked to do the winding; instead, I'd take the skein and trail the multicolored yarn all through the house, "untangling" it and trying to find the end before the thread became taut.

I always loved to hear Nannie tell stories about her childhood, and she told them regularly in alternation. Many times she would begin by reminding me of her history, and then I would listen as stories were unraveled from and woven into it:

"My mother died when I was six months old. I was the ninth child of the first family. Father married again in a couple of years; then in the second family there were six children, so there was a large family at the old homeplace there at the foot of the mountain." And she nodded to the painting of the old home, hanging across the room above the TV. "Oh, we had great times there--laughing, singing--and we also learned our lessons along the way."

"When I was a little girl, I was kind of lazy; but they give me peas to drop with the corn when we were putting out our crop. Well, there was *so* many peas, and I got tired. I dug a little hole and poured most of the peas, and covered them up. I thought I was rid of it. But one day, I was playing in the yard, and my daddy come to me and said, 'Come go with me.' Well, he usually had something nice to show me, but this time we went to the place where I had buried those peas. I never seen so many peas..."

Now she began to laugh hard, with her belly bouncing up and down. We always said her "motor was running" when she laughed like that, and I liked for her motor to run. We laughed a lot there on the couch in front of the window. Momma always said Nannie sat there so she could watch all the neighbors, but I always knew it was so she could feel the sun, look at the trees, flowers, and sky, and watch the birds.

I never knew which Nannie liked more: flowers or birds. I do know that the pansy was one of her favorite flowers. I liked to give her pansies for Mother's Day for her to plant in the flower beds and for me to pick for her in the summer. I'd go out, pick as many as I could hold in both hands, and then come to her on the couch and strew them all across her apron. She'd lay down her knitting, laughing, and look at the "face" on each one, and then find a vase for me to arrange them in.

She also used to grow a few vegetables of her own out back--little yellow tomatoes in particular--despite Papaw's big garden there. Before we could go out looking for ripe ones, she had to get her cane, put on her bonnet, put mine on me, and get the straw basket. Then we were ready. I walked slowly beside her, resisting the urge to run impatiently ahead, and we finally reached the tomatoes, having made our path through the violets and periwinkle growing amid the grass. Running her eyes and fingers expertly over the vine, she'd usually find a few and drop them in the basket after commenting on any peculiarities of each. Then we'd come inside, and she'd wash a few for me to eat. I always thought they tasted kind of bitter, but I ate them--and liked them--because Nannie grew them. After we'd eaten some tomatoes and she'd made her a cup of coffee and poured me a glass of milk, it was time to go back to the couch and our knitting:

"My aunt had made me a doll. She cut it out of domestic cloth and stuffed it with wheat bran, and I was very proud of my doll--until there was a little half-brother born. Father told me I would have to take care of the baby. So I taken my doll--I didn't think I'd need it anymore--I'd taken it and threw it over the fence, went back to the house and asked to have that baby. I thought I could play with it like I had my doll. They wouldn't let me have it, so I went back to get my doll. In the meantime, an old cow had come up and was *eating my doll!* I could only see the legs and arms working from her mouth. Well, of course, I cried--they wouldn't let me have the baby, and the cow had eat my doll. But that had to pass too..."

"When I got older I played more with the other children. We lived in the mountains, so we children had to play and go places in the mountains. My father--to keep us from getting lost--he would make trails for us. He called it 'blazing a trail.' He would take his axe, skin the bark on one side of the tree at the edge of the woods, then go a little ways and to the left there'd be another mark on a tree. He would do that through the woods to a neighbor's house or where he thought we should go. One day my sister and me were going somewhere. We seen some berries, and we decided we'd go pick berries. While picking berries, we lost the trail. We had to wander around until we finally found the trail. This was a great lesson. We grown-ups, when we depart from the right trail, we get lost and wander away from the one that watches us--which is a guarding angel. And that guarding angel will bring us back when we *know* that we have gone wrong. So this is a great lesson for us as grown-up ones. We too are children, and our Heavenly Father loves us still as He did when we were little children. So let us always be careful and stay in the trail He has blazed for us..."

Nannie's daddy was a Baptist preacher, and I thought at times like these that she had inherited some of "it." Being a six-year-old, I liked stories, not sermons (though I knew I was supposed to). Besides, I knew she was a Seventh-Day Adventist and I was a Baptist, and that made us different. I didn't really know *why* she was different. My parents and grandparents were Baptist. Momma told me a bunch of Adventists befriended her around the time she started having problems with my great-granddaddy and then after he left. Momma said he let his children go barefoot while he spent his money on booze and women, and Nannie finally told him to choose between her and his whore. He left. She heard nothing of him until she found out about five years after he died that he'd been living in Florida with a niece. He had no niece. Nannie never divorced him--or the church. I hardly ever heard her speak of my great-granddaddy, but she spoke of her church--and her children.

"I was eighteen years old when I got married in 1900. In 1901 I started a family. And there was a little girl. In two year there was a little boy come to live with us. And from that there was five little girls. Charlie, though, he was always getting into mischief. I remember one day after your Mamaw had just started to school, I picked up a couple of her schoolbooks, lifted the covers, and saw 'shit' scrawled on the inside. Come to find out she'd wanted to write her name in her books and asked Charlie how to spell it." And Nannie's motor ran as we both bounced in laughter on the couch. Finally, she began again, and her tone became strained as her eyes narrowed to focus on her knitting. "We lost two of the children, Audie and Daisy, when they were small. Then when he was eighteen, Charlie drowned in the lake. Your Aunt Alice died of that heart attack when you were in kindergarten. So there's only two left, and of course, they're the ones I live with--your Mamaw and Aunt Mary. Then there was grandchildren started. Of course, your mother's one. All together there was two grandsons and four granddaughters. Then there was more started--there was great-grandchildren. I had seven great-grandsons, all big and husky men, and there was four great-granddaughters. We call our family tree the 'nut tree.' Of course, we lost some nuts but we still keep adding to the tree. We're now in the fifth generation--four great-great-grandchildren. And I am still here, knitting and waiting for more."

Dying was always what happened to *other* people's great-grandmothers until November 1986. I suppose since she'd been saying for the past forty years that she would die soon, I quit believing it could ever happen. But Nannie slowly and peacefully lost consciousness and then stopped breathing--like drifting to sleep, only stiller. The doctors didn't know why she died, except that she was 104, tired, and ready to go home.

But *I* wasn't ready. *I* felt rather as *she* felt in the story she had told me so many times about the funeral for her pet cat, when she kept asking her brothers to "put it down...I want to look at it again" as they carried it to the burying ground.

After she died, Mamaw went to the box in Nannie's closet marked, "My Funeral," never before opened by anyone except Nannie, and found the clothes she wished to be buried in (a gown and robe since, according to her beliefs, she would be "asleep" until Jesus comes) and handwritten documents (dated 1956) indicating every detail of the service she wanted, including the specific scripture to be read and the hymns to be played, along with a message:

For the Children

I request no flowers. I have been greatly blessed
with flowers in life, and I have enjoyed the sweet
fragrance of the rose and have been pricked by its
thorns. It has all been sweet.

And now to my loved ones. I have no earthly trea-
sures to leave you--only that you love one another as

I have loved you. And that you love God above all
and keep His commandments and live for Him. Please
don't grieve for me. The Lord has let me stay with
you a long time, and it won't be long until He will
come and gather us Home again. The Lord bless and
keep you all is the prayer I leave with you.

The family could not abide entirely by Nannie's request for no flowers, since she had loved them so, but Nannie had stated one exception to her request for no flowers. She wanted to be buried with a peace rose in her hand because, as she said, "I will be at peace." Unfortunately, however, the peace rose was out of season, with none to be found. Since she had always loved the yellow rose too, it was the chosen substitute. When the arrangement of yellow roses arrived at last, Mom looked doubtfully at the single, tightly closed bud the funeral director was placing in Nannie's hand and reached to the back of the arrangement to pull out a slightly more open bud. Then she cupped it in her hands and breathed her warm breath into it to open it, finally placing it in Nannie's hand.

As I slowly approached her coffin, I sensed the increasing insistence of the unfamiliar smell that tinged the air. I could not identify it. When I moved close enough to see Nannie lying there, I had to agree with the others. She did look pretty --a pretty woman. But the not quite completely gray hair that had never been curled in her 104 years--was curled--and sprayed. The neck I had never seen wearing a scarf--had one. I stood there a long time and then walked away.

In an hour (or a day) I returned alone. I wanted to touch her...I thought. I had never touched a corpse, but this was Nannie. My mind flashed briefly to my childhood days and the many times she had been eager to share and respond to my curiosities. I remembered her encouraging me to push down on the veins that stood on top of her hands and watch the blood stop--and start. I remembered our laughter on the couch.

I lightly stroked her hand with mine. It felt like clay...and cold--so very cold. I pulled my hand away and saw the mortician's make-up on my hand. I tentatively touched her face. Her cheeks felt soft, unlike the startling rigidity of her hand, beneath the make-up mask. She never wore make-up. This was not Nannie. I knew that I would have to go to Blairsville, Georgia, the place in the painting, to look for her, though I also knew I must wait.

———————

Driving 45 down Mulky Gap Road, barely ahead of the billow of dust tossed up by the tires, I try to imagine the child of the late 1800's riding by her daddy in the wagon, moving toward home. She spoke of this place as often as I would point to the painting on the wall and say, "Nannie, tell me about your old homeplace." But six months after her death I learn how memory and imagination must strain to revive the images she gave me and to search for the ones she left for me to find alone here in the Blue Ridge Mountains.

I pass by the road leading to Owl Town, where Nannie's brothers, the Walker boys, always went to get their shine and a little trouble, intent on finding the turn-off that will lead me to the land pictured in that painting that now hangs on my wall. I must have passed it somewhere, but up ahead I see Mt. Pleasant Church, founded by Nannie's daddy, so I decide to stop there for now and turn around later.

As I open the door to this one-room building, I listen to the echo of "Precious Memories" and "In the Sweet By and By" as the melodies bounce through my head and off the wooden pews and walls of the empty church. "In Loving Memory of Rev. J. C. Walker," I read from the end of one of the pews. And I chuckle as I think of this man who, as a child, read to his illiterate father from the Bible, "Woe be unto the man who makes his kids run in the fields to stop up the pig holes, for a mighty wind will come up and blow him away." After I walk the few steps from the back of the church to the pulpit, I find under the plain wooden stand the pulpit Bible Nannie placed here in memory of her father 35 years ago and am startled to find it identical to the Bible my mother just placed in Nannie's church in memory of her.

As I walk outside the building, past the outhouse and into the graveyard, I see the markers for Nannie's parents and stepmother. I wonder how I missed the turn-off, but I know I can't be far from the homeplace since Nannie and her brothers and sisters used to walk here for church and school. This is the schoolhouse where that little girl stood to spell "cow" and in her excitement blurted "kee-ow, cow" and started for the head of the class while her classmates laughed. I get back in the car and weave down Mt. Pleasant Church Road toward Mulky Gap.

Finally, I see my turn-off in the bend of a curve and twist up the driveway, past where the fields used to be, past where the barn used to be, to the modern farmhouse at the top of the hill--where the house in my painting used to stand. Besides the part of the hill the current owner had bulldozed and the re-routing of the creek accomplished by a neighbor so the water would flow beside his house, the land itself appears unchanged. Certainly the mountains behind the house stand as before, and I can point to the place where the frightened teenager, babysitting her half-brothers and sisters, saw the cloudburst that sent that gush of water streaming down the mountain toward the fields.

No one is home at the farmhouse, so I park the car and walk down below the house toward the woods where Nannie's father would "blaze a trail." Fighting my way through the fog of gnats and mosquitoes, I follow the trail shimmering with sunlit mica. I pass the ruins of a smokehouse and then stand in awe before the still intact cabin my great-great-grandaddy built for his daughter, my Nannie, and her new husband and where my now 80 year-old aunt was born. I enter cautiously beneath the hornet's nest and stand in the larger of the two rooms, struggling to imagine a stove...a table...a bed...and I remember the place setting I have at home that set the table in this house.

I walk down to the creek to let the sound of the rushing water carry me further back into this time...this place. I take off my shoes and step in to wade in the cool, pure rush of mountain water and feel its passing around my ankles, urging me downstream. I feel the closeness of the girl who came to this creek once a month--and fearful--to wash from her underclothing that which she didn't understand. I breathe deeply the cool mountain air and feel it cleansing my lungs and face as the cool water washes my feet and ankles and bathes my cupped hands as I lower them beneath the flowing ripples. I know I am finally at home.

———————

Today I sit in her old wooden rocker, my hands caressing the golden armrests polished smooth by the stroking of her arthritic hands as she rocked slowly and silently and watched the cardinals, mockingbirds, robins, and sparrows feed outside her bedroom window during the mere fifth of her life that I shared. I rock, keeping rhythm with the memories pulsing in my head, and knit, having wound my own thread into balls that feed the thread smoothly and easily to the needles as I work. As my knitting begins to take the shape of a bootie, a pattern invented by Nannie and repeated by her thousands of times, I realize that though she's dead, I haven't lost her; for a part of her has become a part of me. And I close my eyes...listen to her stories and feel the caress of mountain air and water...then knit...unravel to pick up dropped stitches, and reweave.

Susan O'Dell Underwood
Up the River

Daddy was away for what seemed a great long time to me, for the year he left us was an entire fifth of my life at the time, and I felt every inch and second of it as if it were a wearily slow dying ember. Years later I realize that his absence was more of a bellwether for our lives than if he'd been there every evening and morning; every minute was informed more by the twitching space he left than by his presence during the first four years of my life.

Of course during this year I forgot the physical. I forgot what he looked like and how he moved and talked. I ached to recall his features; my face flushed hot from the effort as I held my breath, hoping stillness would make the task easier. Mama hid every picture of him, even stashed away his high school yearbooks and the family photo album. I clutched compulsively onto one strong memory, which had brightened deeply into me from evening after evening of sitting beside him in his big chair, and that was the impression of my hand in his and how it looked as we constantly touched fingers and wrists, as I absently played with his broad, dulled wedding band. In my mind that year always loomed these wide-knuckled hands, calloused and pudgy, his left hand with two knuckles gone from the index finger and one from the middle. I never knew exactly when he had lost these; it was probably in high school before he married. I do know that it was one of many foolish, drunken stunts my daddy pulled, less horrible than some and worse than others, and that it involved taking a dare to catch a high-flung open buck knife by the handle. This hand I had always fondled carefully, silently tapping the ends where there were no fingernails.

While Daddy was away for the year Dunn would sit in his chair in the evenings and push me away if I tried to climb up next to him, even though he was only three then. During the day we spent all our time together in our big bedroom at the back of the house. Mama stopped taking us to church on Sunday mornings, and we never went into town on crowded Saturdays. The drive from our farm into town, only a distance of five miles, became rare, and Mama learned to cut our hair, even her own.

When we did go shopping for necessities such as new shoes for the winter, or for coffee or flour, Mama was typically silent; and at these times she made Dunn and me stay quiet too. The heated hush that filled the Rambler, I knew, was part of Daddy's absence, just as was keeping to ourselves and filling the long days with one task after another at home. We harbored from people for weeks at a time, through the heat of July and August, and during the long winter months, hemmed in by banks of heavy, candescent snow.

During these jaunts into Newport, the men would stop Mama on the street to ask about Daddy, and the women would always glance up from baby carriages and grocery carts and then glance quickly away. Some clerk or other invariably condescended, "What do you hear from Vernon lately?"

Mama always just smiled and nodded, but never answered them, as if she had momentarily forgotten the language or her manners. Her face, as she turned away, hurrying, pinched into a tight, grieved half-smile, and her eyes burned, empty dark stars.

Even at home we never spoke of him. Mama and her mother, Granny Pearl, would only wonder out loud about him when Dunn and I were supposed to be out of earshot; and even then they never said his name, only referring to Daddy as "he" or "him," whispering. This huge vacuum, the space we built to cushion ourselves from his absence, grew from the size of a blind cinder until it finally consumed every corner of the house. Even outside, even in the corner woods in the far field, there in the spring water coolness on an unbearable summer day, the space followed me about, this vacancy more potent than anybody, this absent father that we stoked to replace the one we knew.

One day in late June, after a year of this life, he just appeared. No one could ever recall hearing the car he hitched a ride in from town; no one heard even one gravel gnawed beneath the tires. No one remembered seeing him walk through the long yard and up the hill to the house. Not one of us heard the screen door swing open and bang shut, although he swore that all these things occurred. It was as if his absence had sealed us off and time had stood unmoved, as if we had hung there deaf and blind and stranded until he broke the spell.

He stood there in the kitchen, sweat drenching his brown union suit, the scent of him rising musky as we hadn't smelled it for months. The early afternoon jammer of insects surrounded the whole house, and the only sound inside was the swinging of the clock pendulum as we all stood looking at each other.

Daddy stood completely empty-handed, as if he were a grown man born out of air, out of nothing, not even a puff of smoke to signify his coming. Not even a stirring of dust. Lifted up past his hard blue eyes, his black, rough sideburns, I felt as if I were hugging some stout old uncle, some vague uncle at a family reunion. Mama pressed Dunn and me forward, as if only out of politeness, though she hung back against the sink, drying a plate she held up to her chest, and Dunn wailed in confusion. Daddy stood there, and me in his arms, looking from my face to Mama's face and down at Dunn, grinning and silent.

Sometimes during the next few months, when Daddy talked about, as he called it, being sent up the river, Mama would get that pinched look she had worn when he was away. This look and her searing stares in my daddy's direction soon transfigured my mother's face into a near-constant scowl. As soon as Daddy finally came to recognize this look, his stories dwindled in length and then in number. Soon whenever Mama was home he would take a nap or leave. But whenever she was at the beauty shop, which she had opened soon after Daddy returned, or when she went to town, Dunn and I fell on Daddy, begging for stories of convicts and crimes with a fast hunger.

As soon as I understood that he had been to prison, the moment that one simple secret unlocked itself about my daddy, I knew everything. I knew the place had smelled pungent, dank, knew the food was either unbearably bland or saturated sharp with salt. I knew the guards and the inmates, each and every meanness and nickname and sin, and I knew what it felt like to be shut away. What I didn't know for some time was what my daddy had done to have reckoned with such a punishment. It was several more years before I understood that my father had been caught running corn mash whiskey into North Carolina for one of his pals who ran a still. He had kept it a secret from his family and from my mother, but surely more than half of Cocke County knew of his dealings. For this offense he was sentenced to one year in the North Carolina State Penitentiary; this and the rest grew clear as a blue flame over the next years of my life.

One thing clear to me was that the worst part of this punishment for Daddy was not that his citizenship was revoked or that a year was lost, and it wasn't that he couldn't find another job. What distressed my daddy was that he could never return to North Carolina, could not ever reside there, could never even set foot in the state legally. He couldn't be caught there or he would meet "serious consequences," a mysterious and awful fate, it sounded. That he could never return, never cross the nearby Tennessee-North Carolina line with welcome, could never go back freely and without worry to Haywood County and his homeplace, was what grieved him. The first few months after he returned, with his family changed and too much free time, he drank often, and it was always a sad drunk Daddy put on then, pitifully crying and moaning as Mama coaxed him to bed. He would fall asleep with tears dried on his dirty face, a sweet liquor-sweat soaking those brown prison clothes. He hardly ever changed into other clothes, sitting around every day in the outfit and black shoes issued to him when he was released.

I sensed somehow, even at six, that he had been more content in jail. At least there he had been hemmed inside, sheltered, and not shoved outside, fenced away from home. The longer he was without something to take his time, the longer he felt bound to us and bound to Cocke County while all the rest of the world went at its usual pace and with its usual freedom, the worse he behaved, rambling around the farm, roaming with his hands shoved deeper and deeper into his pockets, his spirit taking a new shape, as a gnarled tree after injury or lightning strike.

Most evenings Daddy spent either drinking with his cronies or out in the barn alone with whiskey or beer. In the early afternoons he spent his time driving the curving back country roads, meandering and losing himself in the lean bevel and swerve and climb of them. It was a rare thing for me to come along because I started school the fall after he returned. But even after Dunn was in first grade a couple of years later, even after Daddy began waiting until we got home from school to traipse the countryside, I was never invited along. Daddy rarely went anywhere alone after Dunn was old enough to go. Dunn was his perfect companion, doing everything Daddy did, younger and more impressionable, more malleable than I ever was. Later he picked up all of Daddy's bad habits, but Daddy was more than glad to have someone in the family with as poor a habits as he had.

So it was an odd thing for me to go with them on their afternoon wanderings, unless I rode with the two of them just as far as town, to meet Mama at her beauty shop, or to stay with Granny Pearl. Even on those occasions, it was a short ride, and I was silent. Most afternoons, the bus would pull to a stop and Daddy would appear in the doorway of the house. Minutes later he and Dunn would climb tumbling into the Chevy flatbed, careening off in a swirl of smoky dust that seemed to cling around me, long after they had disappeared, choking my long afternoons, dimming the very yard and the empty house as I waited.

There is one time in my memory, then, that is both precious and hard to think about, when Daddy took me fishing with him. I can't recall now why he didn't take Dunn instead or why Dunn didn't go with us. But at the time I suppose I didn't stop to ponder; I only swayed dizzily in the truck as we swung around wide curves, knowing I was Daddy's sole companion as we set out one humid summer morning. This single morning and the memory of mornings before he went to the pen are what

I try to think of when I think of my daddy. Before, these were the bright days, the days I had learned to long for but never really hoped for. These are the flickering mornings I strain to heap at the top of all my remembering. This one summer morning I recall as magical, everything with a bright, fiery hue, the treetops an incandescent new green, and underneath the damp, cool, shaking off the last of night.

We ended up, after stopping only for drinks and new line and lead sinkers, several miles from home, down on the French Broad River, at a damp place where a small waterfall trickled down the steep, hard bank. The entire scene seemed to me engulfed in a blaze of mystery, a secret, hidden place one finds only by chance or after years of searching. Anything might happen in a place like this. The world was waking up, new again, and my father and I were settling down beside one another in the cool grass along the river.

He leaned back against a large brown river rock and tipped his hat brim lower onto his forehead, just as soon as we had unloaded all our gear and tackle and had opened a couple of RC Colas. After several minutes, with the empty long-necked bottle in my hand, I grew curious and impatient. I hesitated, as he breathed deeply in and out, in and out, his hands folded across his stomach loosely.

"Ain't we going to fish?" I asked. He was silent, still. I thought maybe he was asleep, but nudged him. "Say, Daddy?"

"Now, what do you think, Sister?" he answered as was his custom with a question.

This always irritated me, and I was more than a little perturbed as the morning grew long and warmer. He stubbornly lay there, nearly immobile. I decided to answer his question, which I knew really wanted no answer. "I had reckoned, since we spent all last night out grubbing where you plowed, looking for nightcrawlers with that dim flashlight..."

"Now, Roverna," he said, raising his cap just above his right eye, glaring blue, "if I'd knowed you was going to whine and bitch, I'd of brung Dunn." His tone threatened like a heaving storm. I fell silent, staring unsure into his eye.

Soon afterwards he started snoring. And at once a vague malaise filled the spinning morning, and loneliness, as I walked a dozen yards or so to the river's edge beside the arched white sycamores. No sound stirred the still air until I began skipping rocks across the wide water. Before long I had used up the few flat stones along the portion of shore I stood on. I faced south, the sun on the left side of my face, and still as stone I waited, looking far across the water for some signal, some instant gesture. The French Broad, where we stopped, was at one of its widest points, and though it roiled and seethed underneath, far out in the middle it appeared strangely still. There was only random evidence of it's speed whenever a small limb or empty plastic container drifted past, moving, moving farther west into Tennessee and away from North Carolina, quickly, out of sight around a near bend. Barefoot, I was tempted to test the waters but dreaded the numb cold clenched around my ankles. I hovered between the perpetual drone of the landscape and the drone of sleep, lulling me. Minutes hung. As I swayed, widening silent circles in the river pulsed.

      Boisterous voices of men suddenly filled the keen air around me, and I spun around nearly losing my balance, craning to look in the direction I had walked from. Through gaps in dense foliage, past saplings I could see Daddy springing up from where he slept to clap a man on the back who was bent double in his laughter. As he leaned up once I recognized him as Sully, one of Daddy's friends. An old, old man I had never seen stood beside them, stooped both from age and laughter, his overalls slack around his bent frame. A silent laugh formed his toothless mouth. I stared and stared into the red hollow depth of it, until he snapped his jaw shut and spat out his tobacco juice in a delicate, fast amber arc.

      His eyes snapped then, too, as he looked up from the ground in my direction. My impulse was to run, but I stood mesmerized. He cried out, "There's a youngun over there. Hey there, girl!"

      My daddy's laugh faded to a serious smile as quickly as he glanced at me. "That's my kid. I brought her so Faye wouldn't bitch about me coming out," I heard him say as he reached for a cigarette and squinted at the noon sun.

      The three of them started whooping and laughing after just a few minutes of talk, and the old man rolled his own cigarettes. I spent the whole afternoon several yards away from them, as they laughed and gossiped on the wide bank of grass underneath the tall sycamores. Birds called in the warm heights above. Distant cowbells sounded, and a few cars pulsed by on the high road above. An airplane droned unseen in the wide blue sky.

      I woke with a gasp, unable to recall falling asleep, clawing around for the familiar. The sky was a richer blue, and all around me was strangely quiet. My head had rested on a wide river rock and my neck was stiff from the dampness and position. The sun was slanted in the sky, but I was soaked with a sleep-sweat. I approached the thick silence nearby where my daddy and Sully and the old man had rested. Our truck was no longer parked on the high roadside above the bank. My footsteps cluttered the quiet as I started to run, but I stopped with a jerk, just short of bumping into the old man, who leaned noiselessly, watching me from behind a tree.

He lunged out at me and I rared back. "Whoa, what's your hurry, girl?" He reached out to me, but I stepped back.

"Where'd my daddy go?" I asked, only half-relieved to see someone.

"Oh, he said I could just keep you," he said, spraying a fine tobacco spit into my face. He mocked my drowsy panic. "Figure we'll have us a fine time. Don't you reckon, Roverna?" he peered closely into my face. A thousand fine wrinkles filled his countenance, giving him an ancient appearance, but his eyes burned young in their sockets, staring at me.

My tongue was a warm stone in my mouth, and my legs stone also. My feet seemed welded into the thick sod.

He finally leaned up, after I had gazed nervously away from his stare for what seemed like ages. He looked back out over the river, not at anything. "Your mama ain't much for your daddy's friends, is she?"

I pictured my mama at home with Dunn. She had looked so young standing in the kitchen doorway early that morning, so carefree.

Again the old man drew closer, his eyes as yellow as his tobacco spit. "She don't much allow him no freedom. No fun a tall. No, not a tall." He reached up and ran a finger along his empty gums. "Now, you better not be tattling on your daddy. You just keep your damn little mouth shut is all I got to say."

Daddy's truck swung into its previous space on the side of the road above. I jerked away from the old man, feeling sick. Daddy and Sully roared through the trees down the steep path, and Daddy was laughing and laughing.

The two of them had obviously gone for some whiskey. Two clear jars burned like stars in my daddy's swinging broad hands. I could hear him and Sully arguing and Daddy hooting and stomping through the undergrowth. In a moment they appeared again, already dizzy. Daddy's wide white mouth was a shock across his red face.

By the time dusk fell over the river my stomach rumbled. I gnawed a raw potato I found in a sack in the truck. I hadn't gotten all the dirt off in the river, and from time to time a sandy grit grated my teeth. I swigged on the last RC. No one caught a fish. No one but the old man had even cast a line, and he just waited silently, perpetually spitting. Every now and then if Daddy or Sully said something about a particular local woman he would laugh that silent, red laugh, wiping his nose on his sleeve. Otherwise he just glanced at me warily every few minutes, as I stood a few feet away, waiting, hoping for his line to go taut.

My knees grown weak and unsteady, I gave up the wait after a while. I left the damp chill water's edge at first dark and climbed on the roof of Sully's car, which was still warm from the day's sun, and parked near where he and my daddy leaned forward in old lawn chairs, drinking. Their voices rose and fell around the small fire they had built.

Sometimes they would be still for long minutes at a time. Silence rang like an anvil around the night sounds of evening swallows diving in the high tree tops and an occasional mysterious splash in the river. Insects and tree frogs buried their sounds in the darkness.

Sully was still picking at Daddy about not getting their liquor at the still he was accustomed to. Daddy finally wouldn't talk to him anymore. "You got to know there's better than this around here, Vern. Hell, you ran better whiskey than this. I'd have done with some sour mash before I'd settled for something so blasted weak. Ain't got no taste, neither."

After this harangue got no response, Sully pulled out another large jar from his fishing gear. I sat up straight, thinking for a moment that they had a third quart of moonshine. But in the light from the fire the jar seethed with green. The sharp edges of legs bent inside the glowing glass that swung like a huge pendant between Sully's thumb and fourth finger.

"See this here bait, Vern. I caught these here katydids fresh this morning early. Only I ain't going to use them for nothing now. So, let's me and you have us a friendly wager. I bet you twenty dollars you can't swallow one of these here bugs." He slowly began twisting off the jar lid.

My daddy looked suddenly sharply at Sully. "I'll pay you twenty dollars if I can't, but if I do, I don't want your money."

Sully just looked at Daddy. "Well, that ain't much of a wager."

"Let me finish, here, Sully. If I do swallow one of them bugs, you got to swallow your own." He looked quickly sober in the light now, challenging. Sully agreed carelessly and shoved the jar awkwardly at Daddy, who dangled his fingers inside, reaching. Soon he had a huge katydid hooked.

Sully leaned forward, and the old man drew closer, putting away his fishing tackle. He paused, his jaw slack, his sober eyes wide. Even I leaned near, slid down the windshield as close as I could get without leaving the car hood.

My daddy dangled this awkward insect over his upturned face and dropped it into his open mouth, grabbed up his depleted jar of moonshine, and with huge gulps finally swallowed it whole.

Sully leaned up and took a slow look at my daddy's face, incredulous.

"Eat up, Sully," Daddy said slowly.

Sully looked at the jar in his hand, hesitating. "About stuck in my craw, Sully. Believe I can still feel him."

Sully held a small, lifeless katydid so close to his nose he was nearly cross-eyed. He closed his eyes tightly; little lines shattered his whole face as he grimaced. He grabbed the jar and swallowed huge mouthfuls to wash down the bug. He stopped, sloshing liquid out of the jar, and coughed. Before he had even finished swallowing my daddy had pulled out another katydid. He was plucking the legs off one by one, clumsily. He took up his jar and popped the green, limbless bug into his mouth. Trickles of liquid ran down his chin, glowing red in the firelight like streaks of molten gold.

The drone of insects filled the cooling air around us. The crickets chirred on and on, and cicadas with their whirring spun out echoes back and forth across the water. At full dark the chill summer darkness invaded the body of Sully's Impala. It was no longer warm from soaking up sun. It gleamed cold. Every place my bare legs touched shot shocks of iron cold through my body. I put my sneakers back on to keep my feet warm, and soon swung open the wide door of the car, crawling inside, sleepier from hunger than anything else. The old man had fallen asleep in a lawn chair, but the voices of Sully and Daddy hummed on. Sully stretched long into the wet grass, and Daddy began to talk darkly about North Carolina, about growing up. I could hear him clearly through the trees, his voice filling up the night. I carefully, slowly shut the wide car door.

I climbed over the dark clothes and bulky gear in Sully's front seat. An odd odor rose from the floorboard. My body fit snugly among the items cluttering the car, my feet beside the steering wheel, my legs scratched with the raw stuffing coming out of the upholstery.

It seemed I had slept only for a few moments when I heard the car door creak open, and huge hands fumbled at my legs. I sat up and yelled, shocked, discovering then my daddy's face, and asked breathlessly, "What?"

"We're going for a little boat ride," he said, drunkenly, but fully aware.

"I thought you all fell asleep."

"Naw, we went and got us a john boat. Come on Sister, it's going to be light soon. We got to get us a move on. They's no time to waste."

"What time is it," I asked, finally crawling out of the car.

"It's about five o'clock, I reckon. You been asleep since evening, Roverna. Quit complaining and come on."

We traipsed along the dark water's edge, stumbling, him from drink and me from sleep. Sully was waiting at the boat. I could barely make out his silhouette in the smothering dark.

"Where's the other one?" I asked.

"Lord, girl, quit asking so many blame questions," said my daddy.

"He's our getaway man," said Sully. My daddy shot him a dark glance, I could tell, and nudged him to get busy.

"He'll pick us up later on. Now, stop asking so many damn questions, Roverna. Get in the boat."

I climbed into the dark, wooden hull. As Sully started the motor and Daddy stumbled across me, I wondered where they had taken the boat from; more alert, I wondered where we were headed.

There was no moon at all, and it was nearly a depthless dark that we faced, as if we were plowing uncertainly into a curtain of black. We headed up the river, east, the outboard motor guiding us against the smooth currents of the French Broad.

No one spoke. My eyes hurt from peering into the black, straining to see. Sully was strangely quiet and fastened his gaze forward as he leaned from the back of the boat, clumsily steering. We veered in sickening, curved motions. Daddy hugged the front of the boat, and I could only see the back of his head as he knelt above the water, looking ahead into the night.

The sky had only barely lightened after what seemed hours, and a fog slowly, sparsely rolled over the water, suspended in the trees like haunts. I shuddered from the chill damp air, even though it was a June daybreak. Birds lifted in the trees, black flitting silhouettes, their bright calls echoing, ringing off the water, which was black but moving. It seemed we would be eternally suspended there, barely moving through the gloom.

"We're in North Carolina now," I heard my daddy's voice. The shock of sudden words blazed through me, an alien sound in the dark. He sounded weary, sober, as if the drunken exciting aspect of the illicit journey had seared away, ashes now in his belly.

"Yes, siree," Sully said, slowing the boat even further, "we're here."

Silence burned the dark. "I can smell it," my daddy said, facing me anxiously, looming out of the dark. "I can smell it. Can't you smell it, Roverna?" He leaned up further, straddling the front seat in the boat, his eyes clear, two burning blue coals. "Can't you?" he pleaded.

We ran lazily then upon something huge. Dangerously swaying, Daddy swung around to see. His already precarious balance lost, he toppled, and the boat pitched with him. I leaned up, trying to stabilize the weight of the rocking boat, but it plunged over, the motor suddenly drowned out. We were all lost in the wet, black depth, cold and sinking.

I left the night, where it ended at the river's surface, and entered another, the darkest world, and I plunged under, heavier and heavier, floating. My sneakers tugged me under and I fought finally to kick them off. I could hold my breath no more, just as I reached the air again, swallowing great, cold, searing gulps of it. I pounded the water, aimlessly, futilely, slipping below again and then rising to gasp into the blue dawn. As I was pulled under again the noise I recognized was incredible, deafening, the thrashing struggle and kick and ache of it. I sank and sank; the great plunging river tore at my hair, and my hands clutched liquid, always liquid, the black, seething, teeming water. I lost myself except this clamour. It was all that was left of me.

My chest heaved as I tried to keep from breathing, and then suddenly I pitched blindly into stones, up onto footholds covered with slick moss. I grasped and stumbled up out of the deep, crawled onto the muddy shore. Crouched there I heaved and heaved in great throatfuls of air. My hair clung all around my face, and my hands and knees pulsed on the clammy, hard rocks on the bank. I struggled to stand up, bent over.

I looked up and around me. Daddy's back was to me where he and Sully stood, bent double from laughter, under the trees along the bank, slapping each other on the back and shaking themselves dry. The dawn had brightened and fog clung around the tree trunks, muffling their drunken laughter. It flickered through the mist, louder and louder, rumbling through me. In the water behind me there was no sign of the john boat.

Daddy started walking away then, still scorching the dawn air with his loud, blazing laugh. All I could do was follow him.

We all clambered up the bank, grabbing at roots and trees. Halfway up I slipped and tumbled nearly all the way to the dark bottom. In the growing light I saw Daddy turn around and notice me. He was still smiling, not at me, just smiling.

"Come on, Sister, we ain't got all day. It's a good thing we got a ride waiting somewheres along here. Otherwise we'd be hoofing it all day long."

When we reached the road above we saw our truck parked several hundred feet down the road. The old man was asleep in the cab. I climbed in beside him, dripping cold. His coat was on the seat, and I tugged it around my shoulders, though it smelled oily and soiled.

I punched him in the shoulder. "Wake up." He started and then glowered at me, then guffawed at Daddy and Sully climbing in beside me.

Less than two miles down the road Sully was snoring into the warm heat starting to fill the truck. My daddy beside me stared straight ahead, seeing and not seeing, not even blinking for long stretches. We soon passed a large blue sign which read, "Welcome to Tennessee." Beside me he stared, still. I sat there, wanting to lean against him and sleep. I pulled the dirty jacket tighter around me and looked into the brightening western sky.

There was the silhouette of the hills, there a far light in a valley house, hidden. There the last star was disappearing.

Ahead of us the sky was bleared grey, lightening and lifting clear. Behind us, I knew, the sun was burning a quick hole in the sky.

Lynn Powell
An October Poem
for Bill

in the river
we find shells,
shed like husks of sycamore bark.
we follow little paths
the sand knits back toward the water.

milkweed nods.
chicory eyes us from the field.
we walk through the tall shore grass
and grasshoppers spring out
wide as the water's wake.

all day this river is a retina
where we float dark as dust
down through the swaying light.

Lynn Powell
At Ninety-Eight

I sure as hell hope the Lord's got beans
to break and string in heaven.
                              --Aunt Roxy

Her mind goes blank
imagining what pearly gates
and boulevards of gold--what
contraption of an afterlife--
could matter more than sweet
potatoes garden dug, still damp,
a green bonfire of mustards,
the pumpkin fattening like a golden calf.
She's lost patience
with that infernal flirt, the future,
outlived the widowed longings of the past.

And though I needle her to tell me
who 80 years ago she loved,
who 60 years ago she nursed,
her loss has turned as silver
and familiar as the moon.
She'd rather go buy nylons at the 5&10,
then, holding to me like a lover,
try on her bright new lipstick, red as fruit.

Mark Brown
Life at Mama Lee's

I went to my grandmother's house a couple of weeks ago and I ran into my past. It wasn't an obvious, life-changing thing; not something that drove me to my knees like Paul on the road to Damascus. Actually, it was quite subtle, and, in fact, has taken several days to sink in.

I had gone to the reception for my grandmother's birthday, her 88th, and had the opportunity to see a wealth of extended family I don't often see. Due to work commitments, my wife couldn't make the party, so I loaded up our baby boy and drove to Pelham, Alabama, a dear place that seems to have grown bigger than God ever intended. Every year progress does away with yet another landmark and replaces it with something--a convenience store, bank branch or dry-cleaners--that means nothing to me. (Like everybody else, I want change as long as it leaves my treasures alone and happens where I think it's appropriate.)

A part of me has always stayed in Pelham and will be there forever. It's that part of me that was happy waving at the man in the caboose as the train passed, that part that liked the penny bags from Shelton's store loaded with candy, that part that still loves everybody like I'm supposed to, 'cause it's what they taught me in Sunday School.

I like to go back to Pelham and stand in my Mama Lee's yard and visit that part of me. I think it's what my dad has meant when he's told me countless times to remember "from whence I came."

I never lived in Pelham, not unless you count myriad Saturday nights when my older sister and I stayed over and Mama Lee and Aunt Susie, her widowed daughter, made hamburgers, the kind where you put the bun in the skillet with just a little leftover grease so they taste that much better. Many an Easter afternoon was spent looking for eggs in the yard and praying the one I was about to pick up was fresh and not one left over from the year before.

But that was then.

Now, time is working on Mama Lee; she tires easily and breathes with the help of oxygen. Time will eventually win. It always does.

This last visit found me late in the afternoon lugging out the baby needs when it was time to go. First the play yard, then the "punkin" seat, then the stroller, and so on, until my compact car was compacted with stuff. I made the rounds of the relatives who were still there and went inside to kiss my grandmother goodbye. My mom, her daughter, carried the baby out to the car and sent us on our way with a kiss and her love.

I put the car in reverse, backed up, shifted into first, and was about to drive away when I thought I saw something out of the corner of my eye. I turned that way, but there was nothing there. I drove away and have had hardly thought about it until just now.

I think it was probably a little boy with a bag of candy waving at the man in the caboose.

A jewel on earth,
a jewel in heaven,
She'll brighten the kingdom around God's great throne
May the angels have peace,
God bless her in heaven.
They've broken my heart and they've left me to roam.

--Roy Acuff

Some months ago I wrote about Pelham and what my grandmother means to me. I walked that acre lot the other day as Roy Acuff's voice haunted me. Having just returned from the cemetery where we laid Mama Lee to rest, I needed time to mourn and moan as I thought about my grandmother.

When she was eight, she became mother to her siblings when her own mother died in a tragedy that rivals Sophocles. In an effort to save his wife the work of toting water from a distant spring, my great-grandfather dug a well at the end of the back porch. The diphtheria-tainted water hit the family hard, killing my great-grandmother and one of her daughters. That began for Mama Lee a life that would well know graveyards. She lost a child in pregnancy, buried her husband, father, stepmother, and her oldest son.

For all the sorrow she knew, I seldom heard pain in her voice. She was brave, buffeted by a deep belief in God and a philosophical resolve to work with what she was given. She was a born member of that noble society called Southern Women; she could have written the pledge manual for every member who followed her in that sorority. Impeccable taste and a queen's etiquette were hers for life. Until I actually knew how poor her family had been, I lived under the delusion that she was a vestige of that grand old Southern aristocracy. Her softened word endings--"dollah" for dollar and "cu-pun" for coupon--coupled with an overpowering sense of decorum led me to that false conclusion.

"Wil-leeeeeee Maaaaae," she would sing to my eldest aunt when she thought her daughter had overstepped the boundaries of decency. Her cheeks innately knew the right shade to blush, dependent on the severity of the offense, but never so great that any moral code was broken. She allowed her eldest son, John, greater leeway in the nature of his humor. Even as a kid I knew that John was the guy I wanted to be: his off-color jokes got the biggest laughs and he never got called down, even when the punchline ended with well-delivered profanity.

John's lost battle to cancer was the strongest blow I saw Mama Lee take. She had been a widow for 36 years and seemed sure that all of her children would outlive her. Several months after John died, I asked her what had been the hardest for her. Her answer, though solemn, was lightning quick, "The hardest thing I've ever had to do was bury my child. It was like burying a part of my own self."

After being her pallbearer last week, I understand--in an inverted sense--her position. As I helped carry her, I knew I was carrying a part of me: both who I am and who I will become.

As we pallbearers stood across from the rest of the family, I thought about the ability Mama Lee had to draw a crowd. We used to gather at her house for Thanksgiving, but, as her children's children grew older, we changed the annual gathering to her birthday in May. Some of my cousins fret that we won't meet anymore because Mama Lee isn't there to call us home. I, however, think we will. It's the only true way to celebrate those parts of her that live in each of us.

Shara Whitford
The Salesman

"I'm selling the Family Encyclopedia," the boy said to Mrs. Cooper as she held the door open, letting the cold air out of the house.

"I'm sorry. We already have a set of encyclopedias." Because they did. Her husband said they needed to give little Jimmy all the advantages in life. And they were; he was allowed to do anything as long as her husband considered it mentally challenging. This included staying up past his bedtime if there was an intellectually stimulating TV show, such as a documentary on the mating habits of the bumble bee.

"All right," the boy said and began to walk away. He looked like he was used to rejection.

"Wait a minute." She made her voice loud and forceful like she used to as an elementary school teacher.

"Yeah." He turned around in the path between the two rows of gardenias.

"What kind of encyclopedias did you say you were selling?"

"The Family Encyclopedia." She remembered that these were an inferior brand to the ones that had already been bought for her son. Her husband said it was never too early to invest in their son's education.

"Well, why don't you come in?" she said. "I'm sorry. I thought you said the name of the kind we already had. My hearing's going." She led him into the living room, a room of pastel pink shades and a vase of cut flowers, and offered him a glass of lemonade. Mrs. Cooper didn't usually do things like this. Her husband was always telling her to be cautious, saying that you just couldn't trust people these days. But, this boy with the bad skin and big feet didn't look like a murderer or a rapist. She never let vacuum cleaner salesmen inside, they always wanted to sprinkle her white carpet with dirt. They tended to look the same, balding men overcompensating with mustaches. Mrs. Cooper, aware that she was still an attractive woman, knew that it might give men ideas to invite them into her house.

"So, how many sets of encyclopedias have you sold today?" She handed him the lemonade.

"None so far."

It was 2:00 in the afternoon and she considered that she should let him be on his way to more likely customers. But, the poor boy looked so hot. The smell of perspiration was already filling her living room, not an unpleasant smell, though. She really just couldn't send him back out into the heat yet. Someday, her own son might be doing the same thing. Her son was only six now, gone away for the day to baseball camp to build more confidence in himself as he was so much smaller than the boys his age.

The boy already seemed to look better. Mrs. Cooper knew how much the heat drained her when she worked in the garden in the afternoons. It made her sleepy and tired, made her think bad thoughts, like wishing she wasn't married and a mother. That was the only time she had those kinds of wishes, though.

"So, how long have you been selling encyclopedias?" she asked the boy, who was picking pieces of imaginary fluff off his trousers.

"Just for about a month."

"Do you like it?" Mrs. Cooper found herself wondering what color underwear the boy was wearing. She remembered as a young wife the pleasure she found in folding her husband's underwear, knowing exactly what he was covering with them.

"Yeah, I guess."

He reminded her of the Mormon boys who walked around the neighborhood knocking on doors, fulfilling their missionary obligations in suits and ties. The boys her husband liked to set the dogs on.

"Are you from around here?" she asked, knowing the answer because of the television announcer accent.

"No, I'm from Illinois."

"Near Chicago?"

"About two hours away." His eyes were on her hands, the nails manicured with splashes of pink. She made certain to wear her gardening gloves to avoid chipping.

"Are you in college?"

"Yes."

"So, this is just a summer job?"

"Yes, ma'am." She hated to be called ma'am.

"So, where did you learn to sell encyclopedias?"

"Chicago."

"How long did they train you?" She thought she heard a car in the driveway, but it must have just been somebody turning around.

"A day."

"Do you work on commission?"

"Yes."

She noticed that his acne scars were purplish, wondered if they would disappear. Her husband had always had perfect skin, judging from his teenage pictures.

The boy began to unpack his suitcase. Mrs. Cooper assumed the presentation materials must be in it. She wondered if he would try to convince her with beautifully colored photographs and a salesman's pitch, saying that they were the best encyclopedias around. The boy unpacked his bag slowly, pulling out A and B and a poster with pictures of the Washington Monument, a cow, and Peruvian women with tough feet. His hands were so young, so free of hair, so different than her husband's hands. Of course, her husband was much older and she had always considerd older men to be so much more attractive, distinguished looking. Men seemed to improve with age. Women didn't. She tried to keep herself up, sometimes even wearing makeup to bed. Her mother had always told her never to sleep with a man before she married him, because you didn't want them to know what you looked like in the morning, not before you had that ring on your finger.

"How much is the whole set of encyclopedias?"

"200 dollars."

She asked the question to be polite. The poor boy didn't seem to be salesman material. Mrs. Cooper certainly hoped that he wasn't using this summer job to pay for school. It must have been a job arranged by his father, to help him overcome his shyness. She almost felt that she had some responsibility to this boy's father, to help his son out, to talk to him about the encyclopedias.

"So, why should I buy these books?"

"They're very educational." He blushed.

"I have a little boy."

"They are good for children."

"My husband is very interested in anything educational for our son."

"They're very educational," he said once again.

"Yes, I'm sure they must be very useful for book reports."

"They are."

"Did you use these encyclopedias when you were a child?" she asked him.

"Yes."

"Do they come in leather?" Her son's were leather.

"No."

This poor boy just didn't want to be drawn out of his shell. She almost felt sorry for him in his naiveté that he could sell these encyclopedias without saying anything at all.

"I guess I should be going," he finally said after a long silence.

"Don't you want to sell me a set of encyclopedias?"

"But, I thought you said you already had a set?"

"Yes, we do, but isn't there something these encyclopedias have that ours don't?"

"Not really."

"Don't these have more information?"

"I don't think so."

"Aren't the pictures more colorful?" she asked.

"Most of the pictures are in black and white."

She picked up the B encyclopedias. "Well, the pictures seem to be closer up. Like this picture of the bear. I don't seem to recall it being nearly as nice in the other encyclopedia."

"Well, if you say so."

These encyclopedias were in a blue cover, bright and cheerful, much nicer than the brown leather of the set that her son already had in his room. She liked the feel of the fake blue leather and picked up the book that was lying beside her thigh. It was rough, not like her son's soft leather one.

"How long does it take to get the set?"

"I think about three weeks."

After the boy left, she looked at the swing set in the backyard. The swing blew back and forth in the hot summer wind. Mrs. Cooper wondered how many bumps, bruises, and scrapes her son would come home with tonight.

Linda Parsons
Rocker

Sweeping today as I do every day,
I moved the chair that was mine as a child.
Forty years of dusting the seat, the laughing
clowns, the blob of petrified gum--and the music
box broke off in my hand. It was mine at four
or five, rocking my bride doll, the metal box
making carnival sounds as I reared forward
and back.

My mother and I were alone
in that attic apartment. I skated round
and round the cedar chest my father
had given for their wedding, their hopes
and creased linens locked inside.
It was where I got over my tonsillectomy
and the lie of all the ice cream I could eat,
dreaming each night of the ether mask
coming down like an ax. It was next door
to the house with goldfish in a pond,
where I pedaled my first two-wheeler.
Where I lay me down in the heat
of red measles, the blinds drawn
to save my eyes, the dark like a kiss
on my forehead.

My mother and I remember it
differently. She says the place had roaches
and on Saturdays the landlord chased her
up three flights. She won't even drive
on that street, it takes her all the way back.
I must've rocked through it, humming
to snatches of a child's music,
wanting our lives to be nothing less
than beautiful, swimming like orange fantails,

forward and back
forward and back.

Linda Parsons
Home Fire

Whether on the boulevard or gravel backroad,
I do not easily raise my hand to those who toss
up theirs in anonymous hello, merely to say
I'm passing this way. Once out of shyness, now
reluctance to tip my hand, I admire the shrubbery
instead. I've learned where the lines are drawn,
and keep the privet well trimmed. I left one house
with toys on the floor for another with quiet rugs
and a bed where the moon comes in. I've thrown
myself at men in black turtlenecks only to find
that home is best after all. Home where I sit
in the glider, knowing it needs oil, like my own
rusty joints. Where I coax blackberry to dogwood
and winter to harvest, where my table is covered
in light. Home where I walk out on the thin page
of night, without waving or giving myself away,
and return with my words burning like fire in the grate.

Linda Parsons
To My Daughter Going Off To College

One day it will not be enough
to make perfect pesto, cinnamon coffee,
and know every little club on Jackson Avenue.
All this you've learned in secret, striking out
on your own. I've said the usual mother things:
there are men downtown who would crack
you open, leave you drying on the curb.
Where will your pearl be then?
I've said, *One day you'll see,*
as you counted your bus tokens.

One day you'll look in the mirror and see
only furniture. You'll feel a great hole
in your heart, a weight in your pocket.
You'll take these crumbs, drop them
by an ancient moon and, in your darkest hour,
find yourself at my door.

I'll take you to the clock on the mantle.
My grandfather used to scavenge the alley
for his clocks. That one's made of bedposts.
He drank, people called him weak.
I watched him work, a carpenter's hands
hiding his bottle when I came too close.
Four daughters, no sons, something less
than a man. As a girl, my mother must've heard
him stumbling in, the raucous chiming
greeting him like children.

Now light the eye of the stove and smell
my grandmother's kitchen. I'd stand shivering
til she struck the long wooden match.
On Saturdays she bought gladiolus
for the altar, for the quick and the dead.
We walked through the hothouse, our palms
brushed yellow for forgiveness.
In the dense geranium air
I clung to her dress like a bud
at the moment of birth.

All week she cut buttonholes
at the Allen Garment Factory.
Thirty years of service,
the diamond pin says.
Up at five, lighting the flame,
her hands planed smooth by the zig
and zag of broadcloth.
I have her hands, people say,
a woman who lived her faith.
She believed in the diamond pin,
in the thirty years. She believed in
his clocks after he died. She forgot
the man who sang to his shadow
and bragged on him finally being saved.

Sometimes I'll turn on the gas, a smell
so sweet I'll turn to hold her dress.
One day all this will be yours:
You'll sit at a vanity, her milk-glass lamps
on either side. You'll take her diamond pin
from the drawer and rub it like a token.
The moon will look new, you'll get up
while your daughter is asleep
to hear the soft ticking.
And with your whole heart
you'll know where you've come.

Linda Parsons
Good Luck Charm

Our hike all done this perfect morning,
the trail extending its hand to receive us,
the mist in slow descent to our shoulders
like the smoke rings I begged from my grandfather
and his pack of Camels. We went the whole way up
Greenbrier, past the swept floor under hemlocks,
the feathery maidenhairs under poplar, past
the little graveyard, its stones as crusted as moles
on a stooped back--the babies *borned and died*
on the same day in 1890, in 1903, in 1910,
and the women who joined them
the next day in heaven.

Driving down from the trailhead, you saw them:
the orange hulls of buckeye broken by squirrel
or groundhog on a river rock. *We need all the luck
we can get*, you said and stopped the car.
We overturned beds of moss and oak for our
lucky charm, the shiny meat with its dimple
of brown that just fits in your palm. But the bank
was picked clean of its sweetness. We found
no buckeyes to carry home in our pockets,
to ward off rheumatism and old age and keep
the dark nights away.

Over the years we've walked this trail, at times
the exhaustions of love weighing down our pockets.
Though once you peeled back a nest of trillium
to show me Indian pipes, pale and shy in their beauty.
And once I showed you a white mushroom hiding
in the paper roots of birch. It rose as simply as this
perfect morning, beautiful in its maleness, fitting
like you in my palm when you take away
the dark night, bringing me
all the luck I need.

SOME NOTES ON AUTHORS

JAMES AGEE was born in Knoxville, Tennessee in 1909 and was educated at St. Andrew's, a boarding school operated under the Monastic order of the Holy Cross. He also attended Phillips Exeter Academy in New Hampshire and Harvard University. He is best known for his powerful sociological study *Let Us Now Praise Famous Men* and for *A Death in the Family*, awarded the Pulitzer Prize posthumously. James Agee died in 1955. He is now known as one of the best creative writers of this century and as perhaps the foremost film critic of his time.

VICTORIA BARKER is a native of Louisville, Kentucky and a graduate of Carson-Newman College (B.A.) and of the University of Tennessee, Knoxville (M.A., Ph.D.). She teaches in the English Department at Carson-Newman College. Her poetry, which most recently appeared in *Appalachian Heritage*, has been influenced by her time spent on the family farm in the mountains of Eastern Kentucky.

RICK BASS is a widely acclaimed environmentalist and naturalist writer and is the author of several prize-winning works of fiction and nonfiction, including *Winter Notes from Montana* and *The Watch*. He was born in Texas, has worked in Mississippi for a time, and presently lives on a remote ranch in northern Montana.

WENDELL BERRY was born in Louisville, Kentucky in 1934. He received both his B.A. and M.A. from the University of Kentucky. He is known as an outstanding poet and essayist and is a spokesperson for conservation, common sense, and sustainable agriculture. His writings celebrate the beauty, power, and peace of nature and the need to respect and foster our relationship with the natural world. He is a fellow of both the Guggenheim Foundation and the Rockefeller Foundation and has been honored for his writings by the National Institute of Arts and Letters. He lives with his family in Port Royal, Kentucky, and he is a member of the faculty at the University of Kentucky.

WILLIAM BLEVINS received degrees from Carson-Newman College, the University of Tennessee, New Orleans Baptist Theological Seminary, and Southern Baptist Theological Seminary. He currently is Professor of Counseling in the Graduate Studies Department at Carson-Newman, and he owns, directs, and provides counseling at the Barnabas Counseling Center, a private counseling center in Jefferson City, TN. His book *Your Family/Your Self* was published by New Harbinger Publications in 1993.

MARK BROWN is a native Alabamian. He received his bachelor's degree in Journalism from Samford University (1986) and his master's in English from the University of Montevallo (1992). He is currently completing the Master in Theological Studies degree from Beeson

Divinity School. He is adjunct English instructor and Director of On-line Services at Carson-Newman College.

KATHRYN STRIPLING BYER is poet-in-residence at Western Carolina University in Cullowhee, North Carolina, and is author of the poetry collection *The Girl in the Midst of the Harvest*. Her volume entitled *Wildwood Flower* is the 1992 Lamont Poetry Selection of The Academy of American Poets.

FRED CHAPPELL is a native of Canton, North Carolina. He received his undergraduate and graduate degrees at Duke University and has been awarded a number of honors for his writings, including the Bollinger Prize in Poetry from Yale University. His works include both fictional writings and poetry which draw from his experiences in the North Carolina mountains. He is currently a professor at the University of North Carolina at Greensboro. Fred Chappell is known as one of the most powerful and influential writers of Appalachia, and he has been a leading voice of Arts and Letters in the region.

WILMA DYKEMAN is a celebrated writer and historian of Appalachia whose numerous and varied works include the outstanding novel *The Tall Woman;* a writer's book of essays, *Explorations;* an award-winning book (with James Stokely) on peace and race relations and civil liberties, *Neither Black Nor White;* and the historical work *Tennessee: A Bicentennial History*. She has been a weekly editor for the *Knoxville News-Sentinel* and has written for several national magazines. She currently makes her home between Newport, Tennessee and Asheville, North Carolina.

DENISE GIARDINA was born in Bluefield, West Virginia, and grew up in a coal camp in McDowell County, where her father was a bookkeeper for a coal company. She attended West Virginia Wesleyan College and the Virginia Theological Center in Alexandria. Her first novel, the critically acclaimed *GoodKing Harry,* is historical in nature, and her second novel, *Storming Heaven,* has been critically acclaimed for its powerful portrayal of the lives and conflicts of the people of the coal camps during the sixties. She lives in Prestonburg, Kentucky.

MARY BOZEMAN HODGES was born in Jefferson City, Tennessee and was educated at Washington University in St. Louis and at the University of Tennessee, Knoxville, where she completed her graduate studies. She currently resides in Jefferson City and teaches at Carson-Newman College in the English Department. Her first novel (unpublished) is based on her experiences growing up in a mining community and is also heavily influenced by the stories told to her by her father and her friends.

BARBARA KINGSOLVER is the author of a number of noted books, including *Animal Dreams, The Bean Trees, Pigs in Heaven,* and *Homeland and Other Stories.* She grew up in eastern Kentucky and presently lives in Tucson, Arizona.

PARKS LANIER is a professor in the English Department at Radford College in Radford, Virginia. He is the author of a chapbook entitled *Appalachian Georgics* and is the editor of a book entitled *The Poetics of Appalachian Space.*

GEORGE ELLA LYON was born in Harlan, Kentucky. She earned her B.A. from Centre College and her M.A. from the University of Arkansas. In 1978 she earned her Ph.D. from Indiana University. She won the Lamont Hall Award in 1983 for her work entitled *Mountain.* She is a noted writer of children's books and has worked through the Kentucky Humanities Council on a literary program for adult new readers. She works as an instructor in English and Creative Writing at the University of Kentucky.

JEFF DANIEL MARION is Distinguished Poet-In-Residence at Carson-Newman College. He currently is directing the Appalachian Studies Center and museum program at Carson-Newman College, and he is a teacher of creative writing and English. He has published a number of books of poetry, including his most current collection, *Lost & Found* (1994). His poems and stories have appeared in a variety of publications and have been anthologized in numerous collections, including *Contemporary Southern Poetry* and *A Southern Appalachian Reader.* In 1978 he was the first recipient of the Literary Arts Fellowship awarded by the Tennessee Arts Commission. He resides in New Market, Tennessee.

STEPHEN MARION lives in Dandridge, Tennessee, and is a reporter for the local newspaper, *The Standard Banner.* He is an honor graduate of Carson-Newman College and has received his MFA in creative writing from Cornell University, where he won the Andrews Prize for Fiction. His current novel (in progress) draws its influence from the lives and times of East Tennessee.

HARRY MIDDLETON has written for numerous publications, including *Sports Illustrated, Smithsonian,* and *Field and Stream.* He is the author of an award-winning book entitled *The Earth is Enough.* He lives outside Birmingham, Alabama.

JUDY ODOM, who lives in the mountains of East Tennessee, holds the master's degree in British literature from Emory University and is a graduate of the Bennington College Writers Program. She also has done post-graduate work as a Stokely Fellow at The University of Tennessee, Knoxville.

GUY L. OSBORNE is chair of the Appalachian Studies Committee at Carson-Newman College in Jefferson City, Tennessee, where he teaches psychology.

LINDA PARSONS is poetry editor for *Now & Then* magazine, published by the Center for Appalachian Studies and Services at East Tennessee State University. Her poems have appeared in numerous journals and anthologies, and she recently won the 1995 Tennessee Poetry Prize, in addition to *Now & Then's* poetry competition and the 1990 AWP Intro Award. She received her B.A. and M.A. in English at the University of Tennessee, Knoxville and is an editor for the internal audit department at UT. She sometimes teaches poetry in UT's Community programs and lives in Knoxville with her two artist daughters and (at last count) two cats.

LYNN POWELL was born in Chattanooga, Tennessee, and grew up in East Tennessee. She earned her MFA degree in creative writing from Cornell University. She has lived and worked in rural Puerto Rico and in Princeton, New Jersey, where she has worked as Writer in the Schools for the New Jersey State Council on the Arts. She now lives in Oberlin, Ohio. Her poetry has been published in a number of regional journals, and in 1987 she was awarded a fellowship from the New Jersey State Council on the Arts. Her most recent book of poetry is *Old and New Testaments,* which won the Brittingham Prize for Poetry.

RITA SIMS QUILLEN is the fifth generation of her father's family to live in Hilton, Virginia. She completed her education at Mountain Empire Community College and East Tennessee State University, receiving her M.A. in 1985. Her poetry, short fiction, essays and criticism have been widely published, and her critical study *Looking for Native Ground; Studies in Contemporary Appalachian Poetry* is an important contribution to scholarship concerning the poetry and poets of the region. She is a noted poet, as evidenced in her collection *October Dusk* (1987).

PAT SALYER was born in Muldraugh, Kentucky, and grew up in Sullivan County, Tennessee. She has worked as a customer service representative, a switchboard operator, and as a church secretary. She notes that her education "can be credited to an extensive use of public libraries and an avid interest in studying people."

KAREN WALDEN SIMPSON was born in Chattanooga, Tennessee, where she lived until attending college in 1984. She earned a B.A. in English and psychology from Carson-Newman College in 1988 and served as editor of the college literary magazine, the *Mossy Creek Journal*. She completed her M.A.T. degree in 1989 and currently lives in Chickamauga, Georgia.

JAMES STILL is one of the most noted of the Appalachian writers. His novel *River of Earth,* published over fifty years ago, is a classic work of Appalachian fiction, powerful and poetic. His other works include the excellent poetry collection, *The Wolfpen Poems,* and a number of story books, including *The Run for the Elbertas.* Since the 1930's he has lived in Eastern Kentucky in a log house on Dead Mare Branch and has worked as a teacher and librarian for the Hindman Settlement School. He has worked with writers throughout the South and has offered readings and workshops in colleges and public school systems throughout the Appalachian region.

SUSAN O'DELL UNDERWOOD grew up in Bristol, Tennessee. She currently teaches in the English Department at Carson-Newman College. She is a former editor of the *Mossy Creek Journal* and has published poems in a number of literary magazines and journals. She earned an MFA in creative writing from the University of North Carolina at Greensboro in 1987, was a recipient of the James Still Fellowship in 1991, and has recently completed the Ph.D. from Florida State University. Her dissertation concerns the fiction and poetry of the Appalachian writer Fred Chappell.

SHARA WHITFORD received her B.A. degree in English from Carson-Newman College, where she was a Presidential Scholar. She is a graduate of the M.A. program in Creative Writing at Lancaster University in Lancaster, England. She presently is working on her first novel and other writings.

GERALD WOOD is Professor of English and Chair of the English Department at Carson-Newman College. He has written articles on Lord Byron, satire, and American film for various journals including the *Keats-Shelley Journal, LiteratureIFilm Quarterly,* and *PostScript.* His edition of *Selected One-Act Plays of Horton Foote* was published by Southern Methodist University Press in 1989, and he has edited *Horton Foote: A Casebook* for Garland Press.